For pattern inquiries, please visit: www.go-crafty.com

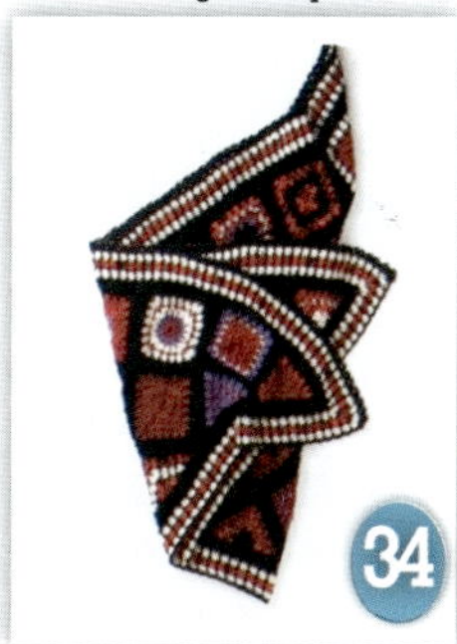

BOLD AND BEAUTIFUL SQUARES

TOOLKIT

YARN (4)
- **7oz/200g, 440yd/400m of any worsted weight wool in maroon (B), purple (C), yellow (D), brown (G), and turquoise (H)**
- **3½oz/100g, 220yd/200m in pink (A), green (E), brick red (F) and cream (I)**

HOOKS
- **K/10½ (6mm) and L/11 (6.5mm) crochet hooks *or size to obtain gauge***

Finished Measurements
Approx 54"/137cm square.

Gauge
1 square = 16"/40.5cm using larger hook.
Take time to check gauge.

Square
Note Work each square in the foll color sequence: A, B, C, D, E, F, G, H, A, B, C, D.
With larger hook and A, ch 5, sl st into first ch to form a ring. **Rnd 1 (RS)** Ch 3 (counts as first dc here and throughout), work 2 dc in ring, ch 2, [work 3 dc in ring, ch 2] 3 times, join with sl st to top of beginning ch, changing to B by drawing B through last 2 loops—12 dc. **Rnd 2** Ch 3, turn, (2 dc, ch 2, 3 dc) in first ch-2 sp, ch 1, [(3 dc, ch 2, 3 dc) in next ch-2 sp, ch 1] 3 times, join with sl st to top of beginning ch, changing to C—24 dc. **Rnd 3** Ch 3, turn, 2 dc in first ch-1 sp, ch 1, [(3 dc, ch 2, 3 dc) in next ch-2 sp, ch 1, 3 dc in next ch-1 sp, ch 1] 3 times, join with sl st to top of beginning ch, changing to D—36 dc. **Rnd 4** Ch 3, turn, 2 dc in first ch-1 sp, ch 1, *(3 dc, ch 2, 3 dc) in next ch-2 sp, ch 1, (3 dc in next ch-1 sp, ch 1) twice; rep from * around, join with sl st to top of beginning ch, changing to E—48 dc. **Rnd 5** Ch 3, turn, 2 dc in first ch-1 sp, ch 1, *(3 dc in next ch-1 sp, ch 1) across to next ch-2 sp, *(3 dc, ch 2, 3 dc) in next ch-2 sp, ch 1; rep from * around, join with sl st to top of beginning ch, changing to F—60 dc. **Rnds 6–12** Rep rnd 5, changing color every rnd according to the sequence above—144 dc. Fasten off.

Finishing
With D, sew or crochet squares together in 3 rows of 3 squares each. Sew or crochet 3 rows together.

Border
Note Work border in the foll color sequence: I, E, F, G, H.
Hold afghan with RS facing. With larger hook and I, attach yarn with sl st to any ch-1 space. **Rnd 1** Ch 3, turn, 2 dc in same ch-1 sp, ch 1, *(work 3 dc in next ch-1 sp, ch 1) across to next corner ch-2 sp, (work 3 dc, ch 2, 3 dc) in corner ch-2 sp, ch 1; rep from * around, join with sl st to top of beginning ch, changing to E. **Rnds 2–5** Rep rnd 1, changing colors according to the Border sequence, turning after rnd 6 and changing to smaller hook. **Rnd 6** With H, sl st in each ch sp and dc around, join and fasten off.

Rose Callahan

Rose Callahan

HONEYCOMB PILLOWS

Jack Deutsch Studio

Finished Measurements
Approx 12"/30.5cm long x 16"/40.5cm wide.

Gauge
Six-point motif = 4⅛"/10.5cm (at widest point).
Take time to check gauge.

Note
To join yarn with a sc, make a slipknot and place on hook. Insert hook in st, yo, draw up a lp, yo and draw through both lps on hook.

Color Sequences
Goldilocks motifs
A bright red, **B** citrus orange, **C** mustard, **D** goldilocks
Mustard motifs
A cherry red, **B** crabapple, **C** ginger, **D** mustard
Ginger motifs
A citrus orange, **B** cherry red, **C** yellow, **D** ginger
Citrus Orange motifs
A goldilocks, **B** ginger, **C** burgundy, **D** citrus orange
Cherry red motifs
A bright red, **B** burgundy, **C** citrus orange, **D** cherry red
Burgundy motifs
A ginger, **B** citrus orange, **C** bright red, **D** burgundy
Crabapple motifs
A mustard, **B** goldilocks, **C** cherry red, **D** bright red

TOOLKIT

YARN (2) • 3½oz/100g, 230yd/210m of any sport weight superwash wool in goldilocks (yellow), mustard, ginger (brown), citrus orange, cherry red, burgundy, and bright red

HOOK • Size F/5 (3.5 mm) crochet hook *or size to obtain gauge*

OTHER • Two 12"/30.5cm x 16"/40.5cm pillow forms

Six-Point Motif
To make an adjustable ring, use A to make a slipknot 10"/25.5cm from free end of yarn. Place slipknot on hook, then wrap free end of yarn twice around your first and second fingers on your left hand. Now work from yarn coming from ball as follows:

Rnd 1 (RS) Ch 3 (counts as 1 dc), 11 dc in ring, pull free end of yarn to close circle, then join rnd with a sl st in 3rd ch of beg ch-3—12 dc. Fasten off.

Rnd 2 (RS) Join B with a sl st in sp between any 2 dc of rnd below, ch 3 (counts as 1 dc), dc in same sp, cont to work 2 dc in sp between each dc around, join rnd with a sl st in top of beg ch-3—24 dc. Fasten off.

Rnd 3 (RS) Join C with a sl st in sp between any 2-dc groups of rnd below, ch 3 (counts as 1 dc), 2 dc in same sp, cont to work 3 dc in sp between each 2-dc group around, join rnd with a sl st in top of beg ch-3—36 dc. Fasten off.

ASSEMBLY DIAGRAM—RANDOM MOTIFS PILLOW

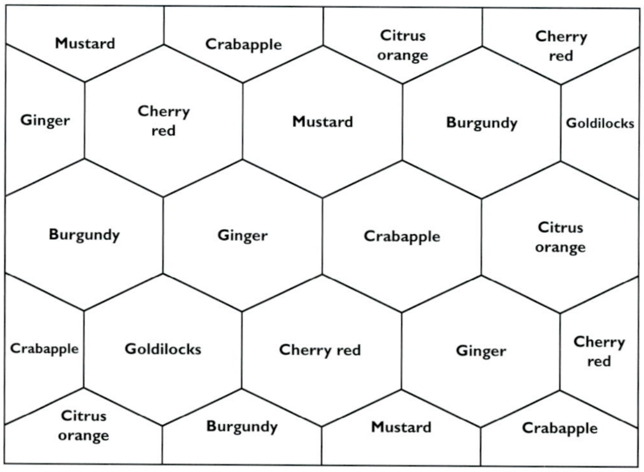

ASSEMBLY DIAGRAM—DIAMOND MOTIFS PILLOW

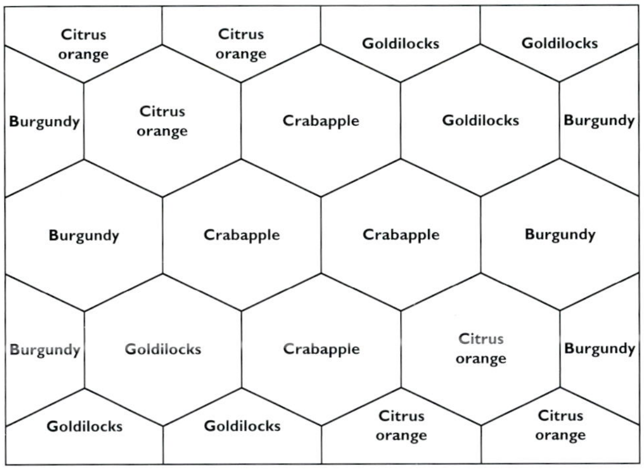

Rnd 4 (RS) Join D with a sc in sp between any 3-dc groups of rnd below, ch 3, *sc in sp between next 2 3-dc groups, ch 3; rep from * around, join rnd with a sl st in first sc—12 sc and 12 ch-3 sps. Do *not* fasten off.
Rnd 5 Sl st in first ch-3 sp, ch 3 (counts as first dc), 3 dc in same ch-sp, (4 dc, ch 2, 4 dc) in next ch-3 sp, *4 dc in next ch-3 sp, (4 dc, ch 2, 4 dc) in next ch-3 sp; rep from * around, join rnd with a sl st in top of beg ch-3. Fasten off, leaving a long tail for sewing.

Two-Point Motif

With A, ch 4.
Row 1 (RS) Skip first 3 ch (counts as 1 dc), 6 dc in last ch—7 dc. Fasten off. *Do not turn.*
Row 2 (RS) Join B with a sl st in top of ch-3 of row below, ch 3 (counts as 1 dc), dc between first and 2nd dc of row below, [2 dc between next 2 dc] 4 times, dc between next dc and last dc, dc in last dc—12 dc. Fasten off. *Do not turn.*
Row 3 (RS) Join C with a sl st in top of ch-3 of row below, ch 3 (counts as 1 dc), dc between first and 2nd dc of row below, 3 dc between first 2-dc and 2nd 2-dc group, [3 dc between next 2 2-dc groups] 4 times, dc between last 2 dc, dc in last dc—19 dc. Fasten off. Turn.
Row 4 (WS) Join D with a sc in first dc, ch 1, sc in sp between first 2-dc and next 3-dc group, [ch 3, sc in sp between next 2 3-dc group] 5 times, ch 1, sc in top of ch-3 t-ch of row below—5 ch-3 sps and 2 ch-1 sps. Turn.
Row 5 (RS) Ch 3 (counts as first dc), dc in ch-1 sp, *4 dc in next ch-3 sp, (4 dc, ch 2, 4 dc) in next ch-3 sp; rep from * once more, 4 dc in last ch-3 sp, dc in ch-1 sp, dc in last sc. Fasten off, leaving long tail for sewing.

Three-Point Motif

Work as for two-point motif through row 4—5 ch-3 sps and 2 ch-1 sps. Turn.
Row 5 (RS) Ch 3 (counts as first dc), dc in ch-1 sp, *(4 dc, ch 2, 4 dc) in next ch-3 sp, 4 dc in next ch-3 sp; rep from * once more, (4 dc , ch 2, 4 dc) in last ch-3 sp, dc in ch-1 sp, dc in last sc. Fasten off, leaving long tail for sewing.

Random Motifs Pillow

Front
Make motifs in color sequences as foll:
Goldilocks 1 six-point motif, 1 two-point motif.
Mustard 1 six-point motif, 2 three-point motifs.
Ginger 2 six-point motifs, 1 two-point motif.
Citrus Orange 1 six-point motif, 2 three-point motifs.
Cherry red 2 six-point motifs, 1 three-point motif and 1 two-point motif.
Burgundy 2 six-point motifs, 1 three-point motif.
Bright red 1 six-point motif, 2 three-point motifs and 1 two-point motif.
Back
With ginger, ch 56.
Row 1 (RS) Dc in 4th ch from hook and in each ch across—53 dc. Turn.
Rows 2–14 Ch 3, dc in each st across. Turn. When row 13 is completed, fasten off, turn.
Row 15 (WS) Join goldilocks with a sl st in first dc, ch 3, dc in same st, dc in each dc across. Turn.
Rows 16–26 Ch 3, dc in each st across. Turn. When row 25 is completed, fasten off, turn.
Row 27 (WS) Join ginger with a sl st in first dc, ch 3, dc in same st, dc in each dc across. Turn.
Rows 28–39 Ch 3, dc in each st across. Turn. When row 39 is completed, fasten off, leaving long tail for sewing.

Diamond Motifs Pillow

Front
Make motifs in color sequences as foll:
Yellow 2 six-point motifs, 4 three-point motifs.
Orange 2 six-point motifs, 4 three-point motifs.
Burgundy 2 six-point motifs, 4 two-point motifs.
Bright Red 4 six-point motifs.
Back
Work as for random motifs pillow using bright red, burgundy and cherry red.

Finishing

Refer to assembly diagram. With WS tog and working through back lps, use yarn ends to whipstitch motifs tog to form pillow front. Place pillow front and back RS tog. Using colors to match back colors, whipstitch along three sides, leaving one short side open. Turn right side out. Insert pillow form; whipstitch opening closed.

SQUARE NECESSITIES

TOOLKIT

YARN (4)
- 7oz/200g, 280yd/250m of any worsted weight wool blend in aqua (A)
- 10½oz/300g, 420yd/380m in dark teal (B) and periwinkle (C)
- 14oz/400g, 560yd/510m in blue (D)
- 17½oz/500g, 690yd/630m in royal blue (E)

HOOK
- Sizes J/10 (6mm) crochet hook *or size to obtain gauge*

Finished Measurements
Approx 61"/155cm square.

Gauge
Rnds 1–3 of Blanket measures 4½"/11.5cm square.
Take time to check gauge.

Blanket
With A, ch 4, join with sl st to first ch to form a ring.
Rnd 1 With A, ch 3 (counts as dc here and throughout), work 2 dc in ring, ch 2, [work 3 dc in ring, ch 2] 3 times, join with sl st to top of beginning ch—four 3-dc clusters.
Rnd 2 Sl st to first ch-2 sp, (work ch 3, 2 dc, ch 2, 3 dc) in first ch-2 sp, ch 1, *(work 3 dc, ch 2, 3 dc) in next ch-2 sp, ch 1; rep from * around, join with sl st to top of beginning ch—eight 3-dc clusters.
Rnd 3 Sl st to first ch-2 sp, (work ch 3, 2 dc, ch 2, 3 dc) in first ch-2 sp, ch 1, *(work 3 dc, ch 1) in next ch-1 sp, (work 3 dc, ch 2, 3 dc) in next ch-2 sp, ch 1; rep from * around, join with sl st to top of beginning ch—twelve 3-dc clusters.
Rnd 4 Sl st to first ch-2 sp, (work ch 3, 2 dc, ch 2, 3 dc) in first ch-2 sp, ch 1, *(work 3 dc, ch 1) in next two ch-1 sps, (work 3 dc, ch 2, 3 dc) in ch-2 sp, ch 1; rep from * around, join with sl st to top of beginning ch—sixteen 3-dc clusters.
Rnd 5 Sl st to first ch 2 sp, (work ch 3, 2 dc, ch 2, 3 dc) in first ch-2 sp, ch 1, *(work 3 dc, ch 1) in next three ch-1 sps, (work 3 dc, ch 2, 3 dc) in ch-2 sp, ch 1; rep from * around, join with sl st to top of beginning ch—twenty 3-dc clusters. Cont to work the square in the established pattern, working (3 dc, ch 2, 3 dc) in each corner ch-2 sp and working (3 dc, ch 1) in each ch-1 sp on sides of square. Join new colors of yarn in corner ch-2 sp and work in the following sequence:
Rnds 6–8 Color A.
Rnd 9 Color C.
Rnds 10–17 Color B.
Rnd 18 Color D.
Rnds 19–26 Color C.
Rnd 27 Color E.
Rnds 28–35 Color D.
Rnd 36 Color A.
Rnds 37–44 Color E.
Fasten off.

Edging
Rnd 1 Attach B in any corner ch-2 sp. Ch 1, work 3 sc into each corner ch-2 sp and 1 sc into each dc and ch-1 sp, join with a sl st to first sc of rnd.
Rnd 2 *Skip next sc, 4 dc in next sc, skip next sc, sl st in next sc; rep from * around, join with sl st to first sc of previous rnd. Fasten off.

Expert hint: While this one-piece afghan might seem intimidating, the large hook size makes it a quick and easy project.

Rose Callahan

QUILT INSPIRED AFGHAN

TOOLKIT

YARN (4) • 10½oz/300g, 600yd/550m of any worsted weight wool in light green (A), teal (B), lime green (C), royal blue (D), kelly green (E), denim blue (F), olive green (G), and light blue (H)

HOOK • Size H/8 (5mm) crochet hook or *size to obtain gauge*

Finished Measurements

Approx 58½ x 65"/148.5 x 166cm.

Gauge

1 motif = approx 7"/17.5cm at the widest point
Take time to check gauge.

Stitch Glossary

dcc (double crochet cluster) *Yo, insert hook in next st, yo and draw up a lp (3 lps on hook), yo and draw through one lp on hook for "chain," [yo and draw through two lps on hook] twice, work 2 dc in chain at the base of previous st, through the face of the chain and under the nub at the back of the chain.

Partial dcc Work same as dcc, working only one dc in ch.

Afghan

Motif A (make 11)
With A, ch 2. Work 11 sc in 2nd ch from hook, join with sl st to first sc.
Rnd 1 Ch 3, in same st work 1 partial dcc, [ch 1, skip one sc, dcc in next sc] 5 times, join with sl st to top of ch-3.
Rnd 2 Join B with sl st in any ch-1 sp, ch 3, 1 partial dcc in same sp, [2 dcc in next ch-1 sp] 5 times, dcc in beg sp, join with sl st to top of ch-3, working last 2 lps with C.
Rnd 3 With C, ch 3, 1 partial dcc between last st worked and beg ch-3, [1 dcc in space between next 2 dcc, 2 dcc in space between next 2 dcc] 5 times, 1 dcc in space between next 2 dcc, 1 dcc in same sp as beg, join with sl st to top of ch-3, working last 2 lps with A.
Rnd 4 With A, ch 3, 1 partial dcc between last st worked and beg ch-3, *[1 dcc in space between next 2 dcc] twice, 2 dcc in space between next 2 dcc; rep from * 4 times more, [1 dcc in space between next 2 dcc] twice, partial dcc in beg st, join with sl st to top of ch-3, working last 2 lps with B.
Rnd 5 With B, sl st in next st, ch 3, 1 partial dcc between last st worked and beg ch-3, *[1 dcc in space between next 2 dcc] 3 times, 2 dcc in space between next 2 dcc; rep from *4 times more, [1 dcc in space between next 2 dcc] 3 times, partial dcc in beg st, join with sl st to top of ch-3. Fasten off.
Motif B (make 11)
With B, ch 2. Work 11 sc in 2nd ch from hook, join with sl st to first sc.
Work rnds 1–5 same as motif A, working rnd 1 with B, rnd 2 with C, rnd 3 with D, rnd 4 with B and rnd 5 with C.

Motif C (make 11)
With C, ch 2. Work 11 sc in 2nd ch from hook, join with sl st to first sc.
Work rnds 1–5 same as motif A, working rnd 1 with C, rnd 2 with D, rnd 3 with E, rnd 4 with C and rnd 5 with D.

Motif D (make 11)
With D, ch 2. Work 11 sc in 2nd ch from hook, join with sl st to first sc.
Work rnds 1–5 same as motif A, working rnd 1 with D, rnd 2 with E, rnd 3 with F, rnd 4 with D and rnd 5 with E.

Motif E (make 11)
With E, ch 2. Work 11 sc in 2nd ch from hook, join with sl st to first sc.
Work rnds 1–5 same as motif A, working rnd 1 with E, rnd 2 with F, rnd 3 with G, rnd 4 with E and rnd 5 with F.

Paul Amato for Lvarepresents

Motif F (make 11)
With F, ch 2. Work 11 sc in 2nd ch from hook, join with sl st to first sc.
Work rnds 1–5 same as motif A, working rnd 1 with F, rnd 2 with G, rnd 3 with H, rnd 4 with F and rnd 5 with G.

Motif G (make 10)
With G, ch 2. Work 11 sc in 2nd ch from hook, join with sl st to first sc.

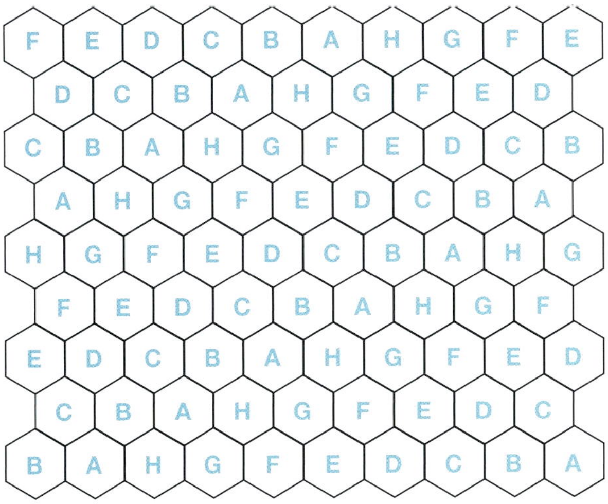

Work rnds 1–5 same as motif A, working rnd 1 with G, rnd 2 with H, rnd 3 with A, rnd 4 with G and rnd 5 with H.

Motif H (make 10)
With H, ch 2. Work 11 sc in 2nd ch from hook, join with sl st to first sc.
Work rnds 1–5 same as motif A, working rnd 1 with H, rnd 2 with A, rnd 3 with B, rnd 4 with H and rnd 5 with A.

Finishing

Foll diagram, using photo as a guide, and using colors as desired, join motifs tog using sc.

VIBRANT SUNRISE AFGHAN

TOOLKIT

YARN (4)
- **12oz/340g, 670yd/620m of any worsted weight superwash wool in variegated orange (A) and red (D)**
- **8oz/226g, 440yd/410m in beige (B), gold (C), and brick red (E)**

HOOK
- **Size J/10 (6mm) crochet hook or** ***size to obtain gauge***

Finished Measurements
Approx 54"/137cm square.

Gauge
1 square = 8¼"/21cm using larger hook.
Take time to check gauge.

Squares
Make 36 squares as foll: 10 squares in A; 4 squares in B; 6 squares in C; 10 squares in D; 6 squares in E. Ch 6, sl st into first ch to form ring.

Rnd 1 (RS) Ch 3 (counts as first dc here and throughout), work 4 dc in ring, ch 2,] work 5 dc in ring, ch 2] 3 times, join with sl st to top of beginning ch—20 dc.

Rnd 2 Ch 3, turn, *(dc, ch 3, dc) in next ch-2 sp, (dc in next dc, ch 1, skip next dc) twice**, dc in next dc; rep from * around ending at **, join with sl st to top of beginning ch—20 dc and 12 ch-3 spaces.

Rnd 3 Ch 3, turn, *dc in each ch-1 sp and each dc across to next ch-3 sp, (2 dc, ch 2, 2 dc) in ch-3 sp; rep from * around, end with dc in next dc, join with sl st to top of beginning ch—44 dc and 4 ch-2 spaces.

Rnd 4 Ch 4 (counts as first dc and ch-1 sp throughout), turn, skip next dc, dc in next dc, ch 1, skip next dc, *(dc, ch 3, dc) in next ch-2 sp, (ch 1, skip next dc, dc in next dc) across to next ch-2 sp, ch 1; rep from * around, join with sl st to 3rd ch of beginning ch—28 dc and 28 chain spaces.

Rnd 5 Rep rnd 3—68 dc and 4 ch-2 spaces.

Rnds 6 and 7 Ch 3, turn, *dc in each dc across to next ch-2 sp, (2 dc, ch 2, 2 dc) in next ch-2 sp; rep from * around, end with dc in each dc to end of rnd, join with sl st to top of beginning ch—100 dc and 4 ch-2 spaces. Fasten off.

Finishing
Sew or crochet squares together following diagram.

Border

With WS facing, attach B with sl st to ch-2 sp of any outer corner.

Rnd 1 Ch 4, along one side edge, work as foll: *[(skip next dc, dc in next dc, ch 1) across to next ch-2 sp, (dc, ch 1) in next 2 ch-2 sp] across to next outer corner ch-2 sp, (dc, ch 3, dc, ch 1) in next outer ch-2 sp; rep from * along the three other sides, ending with (dc, ch 3) in first corner ch-2 sp, join with sl st to top of beginning ch, changing to C by drawing C through last 2 loops. **Rnd 2** Ch 3, turn, *(2 dc, ch 2, 2 dc) in next ch-3 sp, dc in each ch-1 sp and dc across to next ch-3 sp; rep from * around, join with sl st to top of beginning ch, changing to A. **Rnd 3** Ch 3, turn, dc in each dc across to next ch-3 sp, (2 dc, ch 2, 2 dc) in next ch-3 sp; rep from * around, end dc in last 2 dc, join with sl st to top of beginning ch and next dc, changing to D. **Rnd 4** Ch 4, turn, skip next dc, (dc in next dc, ch 1, skip next dc) across to next ch-2 sp, *(dc, ch 3, dc) in next ch-2 sp, (ch 1, skip next dc, dc in next dc) across to next ch-2 sp, ch 1; rep from * around, join with sl st to top of beginning ch, changing to E. **Rnd 5** Ch 3, turn, *dc in each ch-1 sp and dc across to next ch-3 sp**, (2 dc, ch 2, 2 dc) in next ch-3 sp; rep from * around ending at **, join with sl st to top of beginning ch. Fasten off.

A	B	C	A	D	E
B	C	A	D	E	D
C	A	D	E	D	A
A	D	E	D	A	C
D	E	D	A	C	B
E	D	A	C	B	A

Rose Callahan

PAGE 11

COUNTRY AFGHAN

TOOLKIT

YARN (4)
- **10½oz/300g, 500yd/460m of any worsted weight wool in burnt orange (B), burgundy (C), and dark brown (F)**
- **7oz/200g, 340yd/310m of any worsted weight wool yarn in yellow (A), taupe (D), blue (E), and green (G)**

HOOKS
- **Sizes H/8 and I/9 (5 and 5.5mm) crochet hooks or *sizes to obtain gauges***

Finished Measurements
Approx 55½"/141cm wide x 55½"/141cm long.

Gauges
4 rnds to 5"/12.5cm over dc motif.
11 sts and 6 rows to 3"/7.5cm over dc border.
Take time to check gauges.

Color Sequence
*2 rnds (or rows) each A, B, C, D, E, F, G; rep from * for color sequence.

Center Motif
With larger hook and A, ch 3. Join ch with a sl st, forming a ring.

Rnd 1 (RS) Ch 3 (counts as 1 dc), 2 dc in ring, ch 3, [3 dc in ring, ch 3] 3 times, join rnd with a sl st in top of beg ch-3—4 corner ch-3 sps.

Rnd 2 Sl st to first corner ch-3 sp, ch 3 (counts as 1 dc), in same ch-sp work (2 dc, ch 3, 3 dc—beg corner made), ch 1, *(3 dc, ch 3, 3 dc) in next ch-3 sp, ch 1; rep from * around twice more, join rnd with a sl st in top of beg ch-3. Fasten off.

Rnd 3 (RS) Join B with a sl st in any corner ch-3 sp, ch 3, in same ch-sp work (2 dc, ch 3, 3 dc), ch 1, 3 dc in next ch-1 sp, ch 1, *(3 dc, ch 3, 3 dc) in next corner ch-3 sp, ch 1, 3 dc in next ch-1 sp, ch 1; rep from * around twice more, join rnd with a sl st in top of beg ch-3.

Rnd 4 Sl st to first corner ch-3 sp, ch 3, in same ch-sp work (2 dc, ch 3, 3 dc), ch 1, [3 dc in next ch-1 sp, ch 1] twice, *(3 dc, ch 3, 3 dc) in next corner ch-1 sp, ch 1, [3 dc in next ch-1 sp, ch 1] twice; rep from * around twice more, join rnd with a sl st in top of beg ch-3. Fasten off.

Rnd 5 (RS) Join C with a sl st in any corner ch-3 sp, ch 3, in same ch-sp work (2 dc, ch 3, 3 dc), ch 1, [3 dc in next ch-1 sp, ch 1] 3 times, *(3 dc, ch 3, 3 dc) in next corner ch-1 sp, ch 1, [3 dc in next ch-1 sp, ch 1] 3 times; rep from * around twice more, join rnd with a sl st in top of beg ch-3.

Rnd 6 Sl st to first corner ch-3 sp, ch 3, in same ch-sp work (2 dc, ch 3, 3 dc), ch 1, [3 dc in next ch-1 sp, ch 1] 4 times, *(3 dc, ch 3, 3 dc) in next corner ch-1 sp, ch 1, [3 dc in next ch-1 sp, ch 1] 4 times; rep from * around twice more, join rnd with a sl st in top of beg ch-3. Fasten off.

Rnd 7 (RS) Join D with a sl st in any corner ch-3 sp, ch 3, in same ch-sp work (2 dc, ch 3, 3 dc), ch 1, [3 dc in next ch-1 sp, ch 1] 5 times, *(3 dc, ch 3, 3 dc) in next corner ch-1 sp, ch 1, [3 dc in next ch-1 sp, ch 1] 5 times; rep from * around twice more, join rnd with a sl st in top of beg ch-3.

Rnd 8 Sl st to first corner ch-3 sp, ch 3, in same ch-sp work (2 dc, ch 3, 3 dc), ch 1, [3 dc in next ch-1 sp, ch 1] 6 times, *(3 dc, ch 3, 3 dc) in next corner ch-1 sp, ch 1, [3 dc in next ch-1 sp, ch 1] 6 times; rep from * around twice more, join rnd with a sl st in top of beg ch-3. Fasten off.

Rnds 9–30 Working in color sequence as established, cont to change colors every other rnd and work one more 3-dc group between corners every rnd.

Corner

Row 1 (RS) With larger hook, join B with a sl st in corner ch-3 sp, ch 4, *skip next 3-dc group, 3 dc in next ch-1 sp, ch 1, rep from * to next corner ch-3 sp, dc in corner ch-3 sp—2 3-dc groups dec. Turn.

Row 2 Ch 4, *skip next 3-dc group, 3 dc in next ch-1 sp, ch 1, rep from * to beg ch-4 sp of row below, dc in ch-4 sp—2 3-dc groups dec. Fasten off. Turn.

Row 3 Join C with a sl st around ending dc of row below, ch 4, *skip next 3-dc group, 3 dc in next ch-1 sp, ch 1, rep from * to ch-4 sp of row below, dc in ch-4 sp. Turn.

Row 4 Ch 4, *skip next 3-dc group, 3 dc in next ch-1 sp, ch 1, rep from * to ch-4 sp of row below, ch 1, dc in ch-4 sp. Fasten off. Turn.

Working in color sequence as established, cont to change colors every other row and decrease two 3-dc groups every row until only one 3-dc group rem, end with a RS row. Turn.

Last row Ch 3, skip first dc, dc in next dc, skip last dc, dc in ch-4 sp. Fasten off.

Rep for 3 rem corners.

Border

Row 1 (RS) With larger hook, join B with a sl st in center dc of last row of corner, ch 3, 3 dc in each ch-sp across, end dc in center dc of last row of opposite corner. Turn.

Rows 2–6 Ch 3, dc in each st across. Turn. When row 6 is completed, fasten off.
Rep border with B on opposite side edge.
Rep border with C on 2 rem side edges.

Corner Motifs (make 4)

With larger hook and E, ch 3. Join ch with a sl st, forming a ring.
Rnds 1 and 2 Rep rnds 1 and 2 of center motif.
Rnd 3 Sl st to first corner ch-3 sp, ch 1, 5 sc in same ch-sp, sc in each st and ch-1 sp around, working 5 sc in each corner ch-3 sp, join rnd with a sl st, in first sc. Fasten off.

Finishing

Whipstitch corner motifs to border, using colors to match.
Edging
Rnd 1 (RS) With smaller hook and F, join yarn with a sl st in any st along side edge, ch 1, sc in each st around and 3 sc in center sc of each corner, join rnd with a sl st in first st.
Rnds 2 and 3 Ch 1, sc in each sc around and 3 sc in center sc of each corner, join rnd with a sl st in first st. When rnd 3 is completed, fasten off.

Expert hint:

The attention-grabbing diamond motif in the center is crocheted first, then stitches are picked up and worked for the corners and border.

Jack Deutsch Studio

SPRINGTIME BLANKET

TOOLKIT

YARN (3) • *Microspun* by Lion Brand Yarn Co., 2½oz/70g, 168yds/154m, acrylic
3 skeins in #124 Mocha (MC)
2 skeins each in #186 Mango (A), #146 Fuchsia (B) and #98 French vanilla (D)
1 skein in #103 Coral (C)

HOOK • Size E/4 (3.5mm) crochet hook *or size to obtain gauge*

OTHER • Yarn needle

Finished Measurements

Approx 25"/63.5cm wide x 28"/71cm long.

Gauge

One square approx 3" x 3"/7.5cm x 7.5cm.
Take time to check gauge.

Stitch Glossary

Cluster (CL) 3 dc in same ch sp or st.

Granny Square (make 56)

Note See diagram for color order of first 3 rnds.

With first color, ch 4. Join with sl st to form ring.

Rnd 1 (RS) Ch 5 (counts as 1 dc and ch 2), [1 dc in ring, ch 2] 7 times. Join with sl st to 3rd ch of beg ch-5. Fasten off.

Rnd 2 Join 2nd color with sl st in any ch-2 sp. Ch 3 (counts as 1 dc), (2 dc in same sp, ch 2), [3 dc in next ch-2 sp, ch 2] 7 times. Join with sl st to 3rd ch of beg ch-5. Fasten off.

Rnd 3 Join 3rd color with sl st in any ch-2 sp. Ch 3 (counts as 1 dc), (2 dc, ch 1, 3 dc) in same sp, ch 1, [(3 dc, ch 1, 3 dc) in next ch-2 sp, ch 1] 7 times. Join with sl st to 3rd ch of beg ch-5. Fasten off.

Rnd 4 Join MC with sl st in any ch-1 sp. Ch 3 (counts as 1 dc), (2 dc, ch 1, 3 dc) in same sp—first corner made, ch 1, *[1 sc in next ch-1 sp, ch 2] twice, 1 sc in next ch-1 sp, ch 1, (3 dc, ch 1, 3 dc) in next ch-1 sp for corner, ch 1; rep from * around, ending last rep with [1 sc in next ch-1 sp, ch 2] twice, sc in next ch-1 sp, ch 1. Join with sl st to 3rd ch of beg ch-5. Fasten off.

Finishing

Arrange squares foll diagram for colorways and join together.

Edging

Note On rnd 1, in addition to working into the 4 outer corner ch-1 sps of corner squares to form new corners, work across each side edge of the blanket and into the inner corner ch-1 sps of squares at the joined seams.

Rnd 1 (RS) Join MC with sl st in any outer corner ch-1 sp. Ch 5 (counts as 1 hdc and ch 3), 1 hdc in same sp—first corner made, **ch 2, *1 hdc in next ch-1 sp, ch 2, [1 hdc in next ch-2 sp, ch 2] twice, 1 hdc in next ch-1 sp, ch 2, 1 hdc in opposite corner ch-1 sp of same square, ch 2, skip joined seam, 1 hdc in corner ch-1 sp of next square, ch 2; rep from * to next outer corner ch-1 sp, (1 hdc, ch 3, 1 hdc) in sp; rep from ** around. Join with sl st to 2nd ch of beg ch-5. Fasten off.

Rnd 2 Join A with sl st in any corner ch-3 sp. Ch 3 (counts as 1 dc), 4 dc in same sp – first corner made, ch 2, *CL in next ch-2 sp, ch 2, skip next ch-2 sp; rep from * to next corner ch-3 sp, 5 dc in sp, ch 2; rep from * around, ending last rep with CL in next ch-2 sp, ch 2. Join with sl st t–o top of beg ch-3. Fasten off.

Rnd 3 Join C with sl st in first dc of any 5-dc corner. Ch 3 (counts as 1 dc), 2 dc in same st, ch 1, 5 dc in 3rd dc of same corner, ch 1, work CL in 5th dc of same corner, ch 2, *CL in 2nd dc of next CL, ch 2; rep from * to next 5-dc corner, (CL in first dc of corner, ch 1, 5 dc in 3rd dc, ch 1, CL in 5th dc) ch 2; rep from * around, ending last rep with CL in 2nd dc of next CL, ch 2. Join with sl st to 3rd ch of beg ch-3. Fasten off.

C, B, A	A, C, B	D, A, C	B, MC, A	D, MC, B	C, B, A	B, MC, B	A, D, A
A, C, B	C, A, D	B, MC, A	C, A, B	C, D, A	MC, D, C	A, D, A	MC, C, B
B, MC, A	MC, D, B	C, A, D	B, MC, A	C, B, D	D, A, B	B, MC, D	C, B, A
C, A, D	D, A, C	A, C, B	MC, D, C	D, MC, B	B, C, A	MC, C, B	B, A, C
D, A, B	B, MC, A	C, A, D	D, A, B	A, C, A	MC, D, B	C, D, A	D, B, D
MC, D, C	A, B, D	MC, D, B	A, B, A	MC, C, B	C, B, A	MC, D, C	B, MC, A
B, C, A	D, MC, B	B, C, A	C, B, D	D, A, C	MC, D, B	C, B, A	A, C, D

Expert hint:

Bright, cheerful colors and silky-smooth yarn make this blanket the perfect gift for a girl of any age.

Jack Deutsch Studio

Rnd 4 Join B with sl st in first dc of any 5-dc corner. Ch 3 (counts as 1 dc), 2 dc in same st, ch 1, 5 dc in 3rd dc of same comer, ch 1, work CL in 5th dc of same corner, ch 2, *CL in 2nd dc of next CL, ch 2; rep from * to next 5-dc corner, (CL in first dc of comer, ch 1, CL in 3rd dc, ch 1, CL in 5th dc) ch 2; rep from * around, ending last rep with CL in 2nd dc of next CL, ch 2. Join with sl st to 3rd ch of beg ch-3. Fasten off.

Rnd 5 Join D with sl st in 2nd dc of any corner CL. Ch 7 (counts as 1 dc and ch 4), sl st in 4th ch from hook—Picot made, 1 dc in same st, ch 2, *1 sc in next ch-sp, 1 dc in 2nd dc of next cluster, ch 4, sl st in 4th ch from hook, 1 dc in same st, ch 2; rep from * around. Join with sl st to 3rd ch of beg ch-7. Fasten off.

RAINBOW BABY AFGHAN

TOOLKIT

YARN (4)
- *Simply Soft Brites* by Caron, 6oz/170g, 315yd/288m, acrylic 2 skeins in #9602 Tapioca (MC)
- 1 skein each in #9604 Watermelon (A), #9605 Mango (B), #9606 Lemonade (C), #9607 Limelight (D), #9608 Blue mint (E) and #9610 Grape (F)

HOOK
- Size G/6 (4mm) crochet hook *or size to obtain gauge*

Finished Measurements

Approx 32"/81cm wide x 36"/91.5cm long.

Gauge

One square = 5"/12.5cm.
Take time to check gauge.

Note

To join yarn with a sc, make a slipknot and place on hook. Insert hook in st, yo, draw up a lp, yo and draw through both lps on hook.

Afghan

Motif A (make 5)
With A, ch 6. Join ch with a sl st, forming a ring.
Rnd 1 (RS) Ch 3 (always counts as 1 dc), 2 dc in ring, ch 2, *3 dc in ring, ch 2; rep from * around twice more, join rnd with a sl st in top of beg ch-3—4 ch-2 sps.
Rnd 2 Sl st in each st to first ch-2 sp, sl st in ch-2 sp, ch 3, in same ch-sp work (2 dc, ch 2, 3 dc—beg corner made), ch 1, *(3 dc, ch 2, 3 dc) in next ch-2 sp, ch 1; rep from * around twice more, join rnd with a sl st in top of beg ch-3—4 corner ch-2 sps.
Rnd 3 Sl st in each st to first corner ch-2 sp, sl st in ch-1 sp, ch 3, in same ch-sp work (2 dc, ch 2, 3 dc), ch 1, 3 dc in next ch-1 sp, ch 1, *(3 dc, ch 2, 3 dc) in next corner ch-1 sp, ch 1, 3 dc in next ch-1 sp, ch 1; rep from * around twice more, join rnd with a sl st in top of beg ch-3. Fasten off.
Rnd 4 (RS) Join MC with a sl st in any corner ch-2 sp, ch 3, in same ch-sp work (2 dc, ch 1, 3 dc), ch 1, [3 dc in next ch-1 sp, ch 1] twice, *(3 dc, ch 2, 3 dc) in next corner ch-2 sp, ch 1, [3 dc in next ch-1 sp, ch 1] twice; rep from * around twice more, join rnd with a sl st in top of beg ch-3. Fasten off, leaving a long end for sewing.
Motif B (make 4)
Work as for motif A using B.
Motif C (make 5)
Work as for motif A using C.
Motif D (make 5)
Work as for motif A using D.
Motif E (make 5)
Work as for motif A using E.
Motif F (make 6)
Work as for motif A using F.

Panel 1	Panel 2	Panel 3	Panel 4	Panel 5
F	E	A	D	C
E	A	D	C	F
A	D	C	F	B
D	C	F	B	E
C	F	B	E	A
F	B	E	A	D

MOTIF KEY
A Watermelon
B Margo
C Lemonade
D Limelight
E Blue mint
F Grape

Expert hint:

Easy-care acrylic makes cleaning up after baby a breeze! No felting or shrinking, this blanket looks just as beautiful after washing as it does fresh off your hook.

Jack Deutsch Studio

Finishing

Referring to assembly diagram, arrange motifs into panels as shown. With RS tog and working through back lps, use MC and sl st squares tog to form panels.

Joining Panels

Place panel 1 behind panel 2 with WS tog and edges even. Working through back lps of each strip, join MC with a sl st in first sts at LH edge.

Row 1 (RS) Working from left to right and through back lps of each panel, sc in each st across. Fasten off.

Working in the same manner, cont joining rem panels tog.

Border

With RS facing, join MC with a sc in any corner ready to work across a short edge.

Rnd 1 (RS) *Work 83 sc evenly spaced across short edge, 3 sc in corner, 101 sc evenly spaced across long edge, 3 sc in corner; rep from * once more omitting 3 sc in corner at end of rep, 2 sc in beg corner, join rnd with a sl st in first st—380 sts.

Rnd 2 Ch 1, sc in same sc as joining, *skip 2 sts, 5 dc in next st, skip 2 sts, sc in next st; rep from * until 5 sts before 3-sc corner, skip 2 sts, 5 dc in next st, skip 2 sts**, sc in next st, 5 dc in next st, sc in next st in 3-sc corner; rep from * 3 times more, ending last rep at **, end sc in next st, 5 dc in next st in beg corner, join rnd with a sl st in first sc. Fasten off.

Rnd 3 (RS) Join D with a sc in first dc of any corner 5-dc group, skip next st, 5 dc in next st, skip next st, sc in next st, *5 dc in next sc, [sc in center dc of next 5-dc group, 5 dc in next sc]** to next corner 5-dc group, sc in first dc of 5-dc corner, skip next st, 5 dc in next st, skip next st, sc in next st; rep from * 3 times more, ending last rep at **, join rnd with a sl st in first sc. Fasten off.

Rnd 4 (RS) Join F with a sc in center dc of any 5-dc group, 5 dc in next sc, *sc in center dc of next 5-dc group, 5 dc in next sc; rep from * around, join rnd with a sl st in first sc. Fasten off.

Rnd 5 Rep rnd 4 using C.

Rnd 6 Rep rnd 3 using A.

Rnd 7 Rep rnd 4 using E.

Rnd 8 (RS) Join MC with a sl st in any st, ch 1, *working from left to right*, sc in each st around, join rnd with a sl st in first st. Fasten off.

FLORAL MEDALLION

TOOLKIT

YARN (4)
- 10½oz/300g, 630yd/570m of any worsted weight wool in orange (MC)
- 5¼oz/150g, 320yd/290m in variegated yellow (CC)

HOOK
- Size G/6 (4mm) crochet hook *or size to obtain gauge*

OTHER
- Yarn needle
- Markers

Finished Measurements
Approx 28½"/72.5cm square.

Gauge
One floral square = 3½"/9.5cm x 3½"/9.5cm. *Take time to check gauge.*

Stitch Glossary
Dc3tog Cluster (Dc3togCL) [Yo and draw lp, yo and draw through 2 lps] 3 times in same st, yo and through all 4 lps.
Dc4tog Cluster (Dc4togCL) [Yo and draw lp, yo and draw through 2 lps] 4 times in same st, yo and through all 5 lps.

Square (make 49)
With CC, ch 6. Join with sl st to form ring.
Rnd 1 (RS) Ch 5 (counts as 1 dc and ch 2), [1 dc in ring, ch 2] 7 times. Join with sl st to 3rd ch of beg ch-5—8 sps.
Rnd 2 Sl st into first ch-sp, ch 3, Dc3togCL in same ch-sp, [ch 5, Dc4togCL in next ch-sp] 7 times, end ch 5. Join with sl st to top of first cluster. Fasten off. Join MC in same st.
Rnd 3 With MC, ch 1, 1 sc in same st, *ch 2, working over ch-5 sp, 1 dc in dc of 1st rnd, ch 2, 1 sc in top of next cluster; rep from * around, ending last rep with 1 dc in dc of 1st rnd, ch 2. Join with sl st to first sc.
Rnd 4 Sl st into next ch-sp, ch 1, 1 sc in same ch-sp, *ch 3, 1 sc in next ch-sp; rep from * around, ending last rep with ch 3. Join with sl st to first sc.
Rnd 5 Sl st into next ch-sp, ch 3 (counts as 1 dc), (1 dc, ch 2, 2 dc) in same ch-sp, *ch 2, 1 sc in next ch-sp, [ch 3, 1 sc in next ch-sp] twice, ch 2**, (2 dc, ch 2, 2dc) in next ch-sp—for Corner; rep from * around, ending last rep at **. Join with sl st to top of beg ch-3. Fasten off.
Arrange squares 7 x 7 and join together.

Edging
With RS facing, join MC in 1st dc after ch-2 sp in corner.
Rnd 1 Ch 1, *1 sc in each of first 2 dc, 1 sc in next ch-2 sp, 1 sc in next sc, 1 sc in next ch-2 space, [1 sc in next sc, 1 sc in next ch-3 sp] twice, 1 sc in each of next 2 dc, 1 sc in ch-2 sp—12 sc along block edge; rep from * to corner, 3 sc in ch-2 sp, rep from * around. Join with sl st to first sc. Marker center sc of each corner.
Rnd 2 Ch 1, 1 sc in first and in next 2 sc, *join CC, 1 sc in each sc across to 4 sc before corner marker, join MC, 1 sc in each of next 4 sc, 3 sc in marked corner sc, 1 sc in each of next 4 sc; rep from * around, ending last rep with 3 sc in marked corner sc, 1 sc in last sc. Join sl st to first sc. Mark center sc of each corner.
Rnd 3 Ch 3 (counts as 1 dc), *1 dc in each sc, 3 dc in marked corner sc; rep from * around. Join with sl st to top of beg ch-3.
Rnd 4 Ch 1, working from left to right, 1 sc in last dc from previous rnd and in each dc around—reverse sc. Join with sl st to first reverse sc. Fasten off.

Finishing
Weave in ends and block lightly.

Jack Deutsch Studio

VIBRANT THROW

TOOLKIT

YARN (3)
- **3½ oz/100g, 230yd/210m of any DK weight variegated wool in green/yellow multi (C1), orange/purple multi (C2), yellow/orange multi (C3), pink/blue multi (C4), purple/pink (C5), dark purple multi (C6), green multi (C7), and orange/green multi (C8)**
- **1¾oz/50g, 120yd/100m in yellow multi (C9), purple (C10), and pink (C11)**

HOOK
- **Size F/5 (3.75mm) crochet hook** *or size to obtain gauge*

OTHER
- **Yarn needle**

Finished Measurements
Approx 29"/73.5cm wide x 33"/84cm long.

Gauge
Each square = 4"/10cm x 4"/10cm.
Take time to check gauge.

Stitch Glossary
Dc2tog (over 2 sts) [Yo and draw lp in next st, yo and draw through 2 lps] twice, yo and draw through all 3 lps on hook.
Dc3tog (over 3 sts) [Yo and draw lp in next st, yo and draw through 2 lps] 3 times, yo and draw through all 4 lps on hook.

Square **(make 7 each using C1–C8)**
Ch 5. Join with sl st to form ring.
Rnd 1 (RS) Ch 3, Dc2tog in ring, *ch 3, Dc3tog in ring; rep from * 5 times, ch 3. Join with sl st to top of beg dc2tog.
Rnd 2 Ch 1, 1 sc first st, *3 sc in ch sp, 1 sc in next st; rep from * around, ending last rep with 3 sc in ch sp—24 sts. Join with sl st to first sc.
Rnd 3 Working in BL, ch 1, 1 sc in first and each of next 4 sts, *(1 sc, ch 1, 1 sc) in next st—for corner, 1 sc in each of next 5 sts; rep from * around, ending last rep with (1 sc, ch 1, 1sc) in last st. Join with sl st to first sc.
Rnd 4 Ch 3 (counts as 1 hdc and ch 1), [skip 1, 1 hdc, ch 1] twice, skip 1, *(1 hdc, ch 1, 1 hdc) in corner ch sp, ch 1, [skip 1, 1 hdc, ch 1] 3 times; rep from * around, ending last rep with (1 hdc, ch 1, 1 hdc) in corner ch sp, ch 1. Join with sl st to 2nd ch of beg ch-3.
Rnd 5 Sl st in ch sp, ch 3 (counts as 1 hdc and ch 1), [skip 1 st, 1 hdc in next sp, ch 1] twice, *(1 hdc, ch 1, 1 hdc) in corner ch sp, ch 1, [skip 1 st, 1 hdc in next sp, ch 1] 4 times; rep from * around, ending last rep with [skip 1 st, 1 hdc in next sp, ch 1] once. Join with sl st to 2nd ch of beg ch-3.
Rnd 6 Sl st in ch sp, ch 3 (counts as 1 hdc and ch 1), [skip 1 st, 1 hdc in next sp, ch 1] twice, *(1 hdc, ch 1, 1 hdc) in corner ch sp, ch 1, [skip 1 st, 1 hdc in next sp, ch 1] 5 times; rep from *, ending last rep with [skip 1 st, 1 hdc in next sp, ch 1] twice. Join with sl st to 2nd ch of beg ch-3.
Rnd 7 Sl st in ch sp, ch 3 (counts as 1 hdc and ch 1), [skip 1 st, 1 hdc in next sp, ch 1] twice, *(1 hdc, ch 2, 1 hdc) in corner ch sp, ch 1, [skip 1 st, 1 hdc in next sp, ch 1] 6 times; rep from *, ending last rep with [skip 1 st, 1 hdc in next sp, ch 1] 3 times. Join with sl st to 2nd ch of beg ch-3.
Rnd 8 Sl st in ch sp, ch 3 (counts as 1 hdc and ch 1), [skip 1 st, 1 hdc in next sp, ch 1] twice, *(1 hdc, ch 2, 1 hdc) in corner ch sp, ch 1, [skip 1 st, 1 hdc in next sp, ch 1] 7 times; rep from *, ending last rep with [skip 1 st, 1 hdc in next sp, ch 1] 4 times. Join with sl st to 2nd ch of beg ch-3. Fasten off.

Finishing
Arrange squares according to diagram and join squares with sl st.

Edging
Rnd 1 With C9, ch 1, 1 sc evenly around with 3 sc in each corner. Join with sl st to first sc. Fasten off.
Rnd 2 With C10, rep rnd 1.
Rnd 3 With C11, *1 sc in next 3 sc, ch 3, sl st in same st as last sc; rep from * around. Join with sl st to first sc. Fasten off. Weave in ends.

C1	C3	C7	C2	C8	C1	C4
C4	C5	C8	C6	C5	C2	C7
C2	C3	C4	C7	C3	C4	C6
C8	C7	C6	C5	C1	C8	C1
C5	C1	C4	C3	C2	C6	C4
C2	C3	C2	C6	C4	C3	C5
C6	C8	C7	C1	C5	C8	C1
C7	C5	C3	C8	C6	C7	C2

Jack Deutsch Studio

ROSES MEDALLION SCARF

Brian Kraus, NYC (Butterick)

TOOLKIT

YARN (5) • 3½ oz/100g, 220yd/200m of any bulky-weight, mohair blend yarn in pink (MC) and red (CC)

HOOK • Size F/5 (4mm) crochet hook *or size to obtain gauge*

Finished Measurements
Approx 5½"/14cm wide x 55"/139.5cm long.

Gauge
1 medallion = 5½"/14cm.
Take time to check gauge.

Medallion (make 10)
With CC, ch 8. Join with sl st to first ch to form ring.

Rnd 1 Ch 6, [1 dc, ch 3] 7 times into ring, join MC with sl st to 4th ch of ch-6.

Rnd 2 With MC, (ch 2, 3 dc, ch 2) in first sp, *4 dc, ch 2 in next sp; rep from * around, join CC with sl st to top of ch-2.

Rnd 3 With CC, (ch 3, 5 dc, ch 3) in first sp, *(6 dc, ch 1) in next sp, (6 dc, ch 3) in foll sp; rep from * twice, (6 dc, ch 1) in last sp, join MC with sl st to top of ch-3.

Rnd 4 With MC, (ch 3, 1 dc, ch 1, 2 dc) in ch-3 sp at corner, *(ch 3, 1 sc) between 3rd and 4th dc of next group, ch 3, 1 sc in ch-1 sp, ch 3, 1 sc between 3rd and 4th dc of next group, ch 3, (2 dc, ch 3, 2 dc) in ch-3 sp at corner; rep from * twice, then rep from * once more omitting last group in parentheses, join with sl st to top of ch-3.

Rnd 5 Work 1 sc between each dc, 4 sc in each corner sp and 3 sc in each ch-3 sp around, join with sl st.

Rnd 6 *Ch 4, skip 1 sc, sl st in next sc; rep from * around. Fasten off.

Join Medallions
Join MC to corner loop of one square, ch 2, sl st in corner loop of 2nd square, *ch 2, sl st in next loop of opposite square; rep from * until all loops along 1 side have been joined. Fasten off. Join rem squares in same way.

Edging
Join MC in any ch-4 loop. Work 2 sc in each ch-4 loop around entire scarf, working 3 sc in each corner loop.

Finishing
Brush lightly to give mohair a fur effect as in photo.

ULTRAVIOLET SCARF

TOOLKIT

YARN (4) • 1¾oz/50g,100yd/80m of any worsted weight wool blend in pink (A), magenta (B), green (C), yellow (D), and dark purple (E)

HOOK • Size H/8 (5mm) crochet hook *or size to obtain gauge*

Finished Measurements

Approx 5½"/14cm wide x 66"/167.5 long.

Gauge

One motif = 5½"/14cm.
Take time to check gauge.

Scarf

Motif 1 (make 3)
With A, ch 4. Join ch with a sl st, forming a ring.
Rnd 1 (RS) Ch 3 (always counts as 1 dc), 2 dc in ring, ch 1, * 3 dc in ring, ch 1; rep from * around twice more, join rnd with a sl st in top of beg ch-3–4 ch-1 sps. Fasten off.
Rnd 2 (RS) Join B with a sl st in any ch-1 sp, ch 3, in same ch-sp work (2 dc, ch 1, 3 dc–beg corner made), ch 1, *(3 dc, ch 1, 3 dc) in next ch-1 sp, ch 1; rep from * around twice more, join rnd with a sl st in top of beg ch-3–4 corner ch-1 sps. Fasten off.
Rnd 3 (RS) Join C with a sl st in any corner ch-1 sp, ch 3, in same ch-sp work (2 dc, ch 1, 3 dc), ch 1, 3 dc in next ch-1 sp, ch 1, *(3 dc, ch 1, 3 dc) in next corner ch-1 sp, ch 1, 3 dc in next ch-1 sp, ch 1; rep from * around twice more, join rnd with a sl st in top of beg ch-3. Fasten off.
Rnd 4 (RS) Join D with a sl st in any corner ch-1 sp, ch 3, in same ch-sp work (2 dc, ch 1, 3 dc), ch 1, [3 dc in next ch-1 sp, ch 1] twice, *(3 dc, ch 1, 3 dc) in next corner ch-1 sp, ch 1, [3 dc in next ch-1 sp, ch 1] twice; rep from * around twice more, join rnd with a sl st in top of beg ch-3. Fasten off.
Rnd 5 (RS) Join E with a sl st in any corner ch-1 sp, ch 3, in same ch-sp work (2 dc, ch 1, 3 dc), ch 1, [3 dc in next ch-1 sp, ch 1] 3 times, *(3 dc, ch 1, 3 dc) in next corner ch-1 sp, ch 1, [3 dc in next ch-1 sp, ch 1] 3 times; rep from * around twice more, join rnd with a sl st in top of beg ch-3. Fasten off, leaving long tail for sewing.
Motif 2 (make 3)
With C, ch 4. Join ch with a sl st, forming a ring.
Cont to work as motif 1 in color sequence as foll:
Rnd 1 C. **Rnd 2** D. **Rnd 3** A. **Rnd 4** B. **Rnd 5** E.
Motif 3 (make 3)
With B, ch 4. Join ch with a sl st, forming a ring.
Cont to work as motif 1 in color sequence as foll:
Rnd 1 B. **Rnd 2** C. **Rnd 3** D. **Rnd 4** A. **Rnd 5** E.
Motif 4 (make 3)
With D, ch 4. Join ch with a sl st, forming a ring.
Cont to work as motif 1 in color sequence as foll:
Rnd 1 D. **Rnd 2** A. **Rnd 3** B. **Rnd 4** C. **Rnd 5** E.

Finishing

Arrange motifs in a strip as foll: 1, 2, 3, 4, 1, 2, 3, 4, 1, 2, 3, 4. With WS tog and working through back lps, use yarn ends to whip-stitch squares tog.

SUN HAT

Jack Deutsch Studio

TOOLKIT

YARN (4) • 3½oz/100g, 140yd/130m of any worsted weight cotton in tan (MC), lemon yellow (A), golden yellow (B), and lime green (C)

HOOK • Size H/8 (5mm) crochet hook or *size to obtain gauges*

OTHER • Small safety pin
• Tapestry needle

Finished Measurements

Head circumference 21"/53.5cm.
Depth 7½"/19cm (excluding brim).

Gauges

One motif = 3"/7.5cm square.
16 sts and 20 rows = 4"/10cm over sc.
Take time to check gauges.

Note

To join yarn with a sc, make a slipknot and place on hook. Insert hook in lp in st, yo, draw up a lp, yo and draw through both lps on hook.

Stitch Glossary

sc2tog [Insert hook in next st, yo and draw up a lp] twice, yo and draw through all 3 lps on hook.

Hatband

Motif (make 7)
With A, ch 6. Join ch with a sl st, forming a ring. **Rnd 1 (RS)** Ch 3 (always counts as 1 dc), 2 dc in ring, ch 2, *3 dc in ring, ch 2; rep from * around twice more, join rnd with a sl st in top of beg ch-3—4 ch-2 sps. Fasten off.
Rnd 2 (RS) Join B with a sl st in any ch-2 sp, ch 3, in same ch-sp work (2 dc, ch 2, 3 dc—beg corner made), ch 1, *(3 dc, ch 2, 3 dc) in next ch-1 sp, ch 1; rep from * around twice more, join rnd with a sl st in top of beg ch-3—4 corner ch-2 sps. Fasten off.
Rnd 3 (RS) Join C with a sc in dc before any corner ch-2 sp, 3 sc in corner ch-2 sp, cont with sc in each dc around, working 3 sc in each corner ch-2 sp, join rnd with a sl st in first sc. Fasten off, leaving long tail for sewing.
With WS tog and working through *back lps*, whipstitch squares tog in a strip, then whipstitch strip tog, forming a ring.

Top edging
With RS facing, join C with a sc in top right corner sc of any motif, sc in each of next 75 sc, join rnd with a sl st in first sc—75 sts. Fasten off.

Bottom edging
With RS facing, join C with a sc in top right corner sc of any motif on opposite edge, then cont to sc in each of next 75 sc, join rnd with a sl st in first sc—76 sts. Fasten off.

Crown

Rnd 1 (RS) With RS facing, join MC with a sc in any sc of top edge, then cont to sc in each st around, inc 2 sts evenly spaced—78 sts. Do not join. Mark last st made with the safety pin. You will be working in a spiral, marking the last st made with the safety pin to indicate end of rnd.
Rnds 2 and 3 Sc in each st around.
Rnd 4 *Sc in next 11 sts, sc2tog; rep from * around—72 sts.
Rnds 5 and 6 Sc in each st around.
Rnd 7 *Sc in next 10 sts, sc2tog; rep from * around—66 sts.
Rnd 8 Sc in each st around.
Rnd 9 *Sc in next 9 sts, sc2tog; rep from * around—60 sts. **Rnd 10** Sc in each st around. **Rnd 11** *Sc in next 8 sts, sc2tog; rep from * around—54 sts. **Rnd 12** *Sc in next 7 sts, sc2tog; rep from * around—48 sts. **Rnd 13** *Sc in next 6 sts, sc2tog; rep from * around—42 sts. **Rnd 14** *Sc in next 5 sts, sc2tog; rep from * around—36 sts. **Rnd 15** *Sc in next 4 sts, sc2tog; rep from * around—30 sts. **Rnd 16** *Sc in next 3 sts, sc2tog; rep from * around—24 sts. **Rnd 17** *Sc in next 2 sts, sc2tog; rep from * around—18 sts. **Rnd 18** *Sc in next st, sc2tog; rep from * around—12 sts. **Rnd 19** [Sc2tog] 6 times—6 sts. Fasten off leaving long tail. Thread end in tapestry needle and weave through rem sts. Pull end to gather and fasten off securely.

Brim

Rnd 1 (RS) With RS facing, join MC with a sc in any sc of bottom edge, then cont to sc in each st around—76 sts. *Do not join.* Mark last st made with the safety pin to indicate end of rnd. **Rnd 2** *Sc in next 3 sts, 2 sc in next st; rep from * around—95 sts. **Rnds 3–5** Sc in each st around. **Rnd 6** *Sc in next 4 sts, 2 sc in next st; rep from * around—114 sts. **Rnds 7–9** Sc in each st around. **Rnd 10** *Sc in next 5 sts, 2 sc in next st; rep from * around—133 sts. **Rnd 11** Sc in each st around. Fasten off.

MOSAIC MAGIC

TOOLKIT

YARN (4) • 1¾oz/50g, 160yd/130m of any worsted weight wool in purple (A), pink (B), black (C), burgundy (D) ball, and fuchsia (E)

HOOK • Size E/4 (3.5mm) crochet hook *or size to obtain gauge*

Radius Pictures

Finished Measurements

Head circumference 18"/45.5 cm.
Depth 7½"/18.5 cm.

Gauge

17 dc and 12 dc rows/rnds = 4"/10cm over dc pat. *Take time to check gauge.*

Cap

Beg at top edge with A, ch 5, join with sl st to first ch to form ring.
Rnd 1 With A, ch 3 (counts as 1 dc on this and all foll rnds), work 12 dc in ring, join with sl st to top of beg chain on this and all foll rnds. **Rnd 2** With B, ch 3, [work 2 dc in next dc] 12 times, join—25 dc.
Rnd 3 With C, ch 2, [2 sc in next dc, 1 sc in next dc] 12 times, join—37 sc. **Rnd 4** With D, ch 3, [2 dc in next sc, 1 dc in each of next 2 sc] 12 times, join—49 dc. **Rnd 5** With E, ch 3, [2 dc in next dc, 1 dc in each of next 3 dc] 12 times, join—61 dc. **Rnd 6** With C, ch 2, [2 sc in next dc, 1 sc in each of next 5 dc] 10 times, join—71 sc. **Rnd 7** With A, ch 3, 1 dc in each of next 7 sc, [2 dc in next sc, 1 dc in each of next 8 sc] 7 times, join—78 dc.
Rnd 8 With B, ch 3, [2 dc in next dc, 1 dc in each of next 10 dc] 7 times, join—85 dc. Lay work aside.

Granny Square

Make six square 1 squares in the foll color sequence: D, B, C.
Make six square 2 squares in the foll color sequence: E, A, C.
Make six square 3 squares in the foll color sequence: A, E, D.
Make six square 4 squares in the foll color sequence: B, C, D.
With D (E, A or B), ch 5, join with sl st to first ch to form ring.
Rnd 1 Ch 3 (counts as 1 sc and ch 2), work 1 sc, ch 2, (2 sc, ch 2) 3 times in ring, join with sl st to 2nd ch of ch-3.
Rnd 2 Join next color in any ch-2 loop, ch 3, work 1 sc in each of next 2 sc, 1 sc in ch-2 loop, ch 2, [1 sc in ch-2 loop, 1 sc in each of next 2 sc, 1 sc in ch-2 loop, ch 2] 3 times, join.
Rnd 3 Join next color in any ch-2 loop, ch 3, work 1 sc in each of next 4 sc, 1 sc in ch-2 loop, ch 2, [1 sc in ch-2 loop, 1 sc in each of next 4 sc, 1 sc in ch-2 loop, ch 2] 3 times, join and fasten off.
For strip 1, join (square 1 to square 2) 6 times by sl st tog on WS. For Strip 2, join (square 3 to square 4) 6 times by sl st tog on WS.
With WS facing and C, sl st strip 1 to the crown of the hat on hold.

Second Stripe Section

Rnd 1 With C, ch 2, work 84 sc evenly around lower edge of strip 1, join—85 sc.
Rnd 2 With B, ch 3, work 84 dc around, join.
Rnd 3 With A, rep rnd 2.
Rnd 4 With E, rep rnd 2.
Rnd 5 With C, ch 2, work even in sc around, join. From WS, sl st strip 2 to the last rnd of the 2nd stripe section.

Brim Edge

Next rnd With B, ch 3, work 84 dc around, join—85 dc.
Next rnd With A, ch 3, work even in dc, join.
Last rnd With E, ch 2, work even in sc. Join and fasten off.

TASSLED MOTIF HAT

TOOLKIT

YARN (4) • 1¾oz/50g, 110yd/100m of any worsted weight wool blend in dark blue (A), light blue (B), green (C), light green (D), grey (E), and medium blue (F)

HOOK • Size H/8 (5mm) crochet hook *or size to obtain gauges*

Finished Measurements

- **Head circumference** 21"/53.5cm.
- **Depth** 9"/23cm.

Gauges

20 sts and 10½ rnds = 4"/10cm over dc using smaller crochet hook.
One motif = 3½"/9cm using smaller crochet hook.
Take time to check gauges.

Notes

1 To join yarn with a sc, make a slipknot and place on hook. Insert hook in lp in st, yo, draw up a lp, yo and draw through both lps on hook.
2 When changing colors, draw new color through last 2 lps on hook when completing st and carry unused color behind work.
3 Joining of rounds is in top of beg ch-3 throughout.

Stitch Glossary

BL (bobble st) In same st [yo, insert hook into st, yo and draw up a lp, yo and draw through 2 lps on hook] 3 times, yo and draw through all 4 lps on hook.

Crown

With smaller hook and A, ch 6. Join ch with a sl st, forming a ring.
Rnd 1 (RS) Ch 1, 12 sc in ring, join rnd with a sl st in first sc.
Rnd 2 Ch 3 (always count as 1 dc), dc in same ch-3 sp, 2 dc in st around, join rnd with a sl st in first dc—18 sts. Fasten off. Turn.
Rnd 3 (WS) Join B with a sl st in same st as joining of rnd below, ch 3, dc in next 2 sts, *dc in next st, 2 dc in next 2 sts; rep from * around, join rnd with a sl st in first dc—30 sts. Fasten off. Turn.
Rnd 4 (RS) Join C with a sl st in same st as joining of rnd below, ch 3, 2 dc in next st, *dc in next st, 2 dc in next st; rep from * around, join rnd with a sl st in first dc—45 sts. Turn.
Rnd 5 Ch 3, dc in next 3 sts, 2 dc in next st, dc in next 4 sts, 2 dc in next st; rep from * around, join rnd with a sl st in first dc—54 sts. Fasten off. Turn.
Rnd 6 (RS) Join D with a sl st in same st as joining of rnd below, ch 3, dc in next 4 sts, 2 dc in next st, *dc in next 5 sts, 2 dc in next st; rep from * around, join rnd with a sl st in first dc—63 sts. Fasten off. Turn.
Rnd 7 (WS) Join A with a sl st in same st as joining of rnd below, ch 3, dc in next 5 sts, 2 dc in next st, *dc in next 6 sts, 2 dc in next st; rep from * around, join rnd with a sl st in first dc—72 sts. Fasten off. Turn.
Rnd 8 (RS) Join E with a sl st in same st as joining of rnd below, ch 3, dc in next 4 sts, 2 dc in next st, *dc in next 5 sts, 2 dc in next st; rep from * around, join rnd with a sl st in first dc—84 sts. Fasten off. Turn.
Rnd 9 (WS) Join F with a sl st in same st as joining of rnd below, ch 3, dc in next 5 sts, 2 dc in next st, dc in next 6 sts, 2 dc in next st; rep from * around, join rnd with a sl st in first dc—96 sts. Turn.
Rnd 10 Ch 3, dc in next 14 sts, 2 dc in next st, *dc in next 15 sts, 2 dc in next st; rep from * around, join rnd with a sl st in first dc—102 sts. Fasten off. Turn.
Rnd 11 (WS) Join D with a sl st in same st as joining of rnd below, ch 3, dc in each st around, join rnd with a sl st in first dc. Fasten off. Turn.
Rnd 12 (RS) Join C with a sl st in same st as joining of rnd below, ch 3, dc in each st around, join rnd with a sl st in first dc. Fasten off. Turn.
Rnd 13 (RS) Join A with a sl st in same st as joining of rnd below, ch 3, dc in each st around, join rnd with a sl st in first dc. Fasten off.

Motifs

Motif 1
With smaller hook and A, ch 4. Join ch with a sl st, forming a ring.
Rnd 1 (RS) Ch 3 (always counts as 1 dc), 2 dc in ring, ch 2, *3 dc in ring, ch 2; rep from * around twice more, join rnd with a sl st in top of beg ch-3—4 ch-2 sps. Fasten off. Turn.
Rnd 2 (WS) Join E with a sl st in any ch-2 sp, ch 3, in same ch-sp (dc, ch 2, 2 dc)—beg corner made, dc in next 3 sts, *(2 dc, ch 2, 2 dc) in next ch-2 sp, dc in next 3 sts; rep from * around twice more, join rnd

with a sl st in top of beg ch-3—4 corner ch-2 sps. Fasten off. Turn.
Rnd 3 (RS) Join F with a sl st in any ch-2 sp, ch 3, in same ch-sp (dc, ch 2, 2 dc), dc in next 7 sts, *(2 dc, ch 2, 2 dc) in next ch-2 sp, dc in next 7 sts; rep from * around twice more, join rnd with a sl st in top of beg ch-3. Fasten off. Turn.
Rnd 4 (WS) Join B with a sl st in any ch-2 sp, ch 3, in same ch-sp (dc, ch 2, 2 dc), dc in next 11 sts, *(2 dc, ch 2, 2 dc) in next ch-2 sp, dc in next 11 sts; rep from * around twice more, join rnd with a sl st in top of beg ch-3. Fasten off leaving a long end for sewing.
Motif 2
With smaller hook and D, ch 4. Join ch with a sl st, forming a ring. Cont to work as motif 1 in color sequence as foll: **Rnd 1** D. **Rnd 2** C. **Rnd 3** E. **Rnd 4** A.
Motif 3
With smaller hook and C, ch 4. Join ch with a sl st, forming a ring. Cont to work as motif 1 in color sequence as foll: **Rnd 1** C. **Rnd 2** B. **Rnd 3** A. **Rnd 4** D.
Motif 4
With smaller hook and E, ch 4. Join ch with a sl st, forming a ring. Cont to work as motif 1 in color sequence as foll: **Rnd 1** E. **Rnd 2** A. **Rnd 3** B. **Rnd 4** F.
Motif 5
With smaller hook and F, ch 4. Join ch with a sl st, forming a ring. Cont to work as motif 1 in color sequence as foll: **Rnd 1** F. **Rnd 2** D. **Rnd 3** C. **Rnd 4** E.
Motif 6
With smaller hook and B, ch 4. Join ch with a sl st, forming a ring. Cont to work as motif 1 in color sequence as foll: **Rnd 1** B. **Rnd 2** A. **Rnd 3** D. **Rnd 4** C.

Finishing
Arrange motifs in a strip as foll: 1, 2, 3, 4, 5, 6. With WS tog and working through back lps, use yarn ends to whipstitch squares tog in a strip, then whipstitch strip tog forming the hatband. Position joining seam of crown over seam of motifs 5 and 6, then using B, whipstitch bottom edge of crown to hatband.

Bottom Band
With RS of hatband facing and smaller hook, join A with a sl st in seam of motifs 5 and 6.
Rnd 1 (RS) Ch 1, 90 sc evenly spaced around entire bottom edge, join rnd with a sl st in first sc. Turn.
Rnd 2 (WS) Ch1, sc in first and in each sc around, join rnd with a sl st in first sc. Turn.
Rnd 3 Ch 3, dc in next 3 sts, **with* D, BL in next st, with A, dc in next 4 sts; rep from * around, end with D, BL in next st, join rnd with a sl st in first st. Turn.
Rnd 4 Ch 1, sc in each st around, join rnd with a sl st in first st. Turn.
Rnd 5 (RS) Ch 1, *working from left to right*, sc in each st around, join rnd with a sl st in first st.

Jack Deutsch Studio

Fasten off.
Braids
For each braid cut two 36"/91.5cm strands of each color. Gather strands tog, ends even. Fold strands in half. On WS, insert larger hook from front to back between 2 dc through bottom band (above seam of motifs 1 and 6). Pull folded yarn through, then draw ends through fold and tighten. Divide strands into 3 equal bundles and braid for 3½"/9cm. Tie ends in a overhand knot. Rep for opposite side of hat, positioning braid above seam of motifs 3 and 4.

QUILTED HAT EFFECT

TOOLKIT

YARN (4) • 4oz/113g, 220yd/200m of any worsted weight cotton/wool blend in pink (A), lavender (B), red(C), and blue (D)

HOOK • Size D/4 (3mm) crochet hook or *size to obtain gauge*

Finished Measurements

Head circumference 21"/53cm.
Depth 7¾"/19.5cm.

Gauge

One motif = 2¾"/7cm across between the points.
Take time to check gauge.

Hat

Motif 1 (make 4)
Row 1 (RS) With C, ch 3, join with sl st to first ch to form ring.
Rnd 1 Ch 1, work 6 sc in ring, join with sl st to first st on this and all foll rnds.
Cut C.
Rnd 2 Join A with sl st in any sc, ch 2 (yo and draw up a loop) twice in same sc, yo and draw through all loops on hook and ch 1 for beg cluster, ch 2 (yo and draw up a loop) 3 times in same sc as beg cluster, yo and through all loops on hook and ch 1 (for cluster), *(work cluster, ch 2, cluster) in next sc; rep from * 4 times more, join to top of first cluster. Cut A.
Rnd 3 Join D with sl st in any ch-2 space, ch 1 (1 sc, ch 2, 1 sc) in same space as sl st, * 3 sc between next 2 clusters, (1 sc, ch 2, 1 sc) in next ch-2 space; rep from* 4 times more, end 3 sc between next 2 clusters, join. Cut D.
Rnd 4 Join A with sl st in any ch-2 space, ch 1, (1 sc, ch 2, 1 sc) in same space as sl st, * 1 sc in each of next 5 sc, (1 sc, ch 2, 1 sc) in next ch-2 space; rep from * 4 times more, end 1 sc in each of last 5 sc. Join and fasten off.
Motif 2 (make 4)
Work as for motif 1, only work rnd 1 with B, rnd 2 with D, rnd 3 with C and rnd 4 with D.
Motif 3 (make 5)
With A, ch 3, join with sl st to form ring.
Rnd 1 Ch 2, work 12 hdc in ring, join to first hdc. Cut A.
Rnd 2 Join C with sl st to any hdc, ch 1, 2 sc in same st with sl st, 2 sc in each of next 11 hdc, join D with sl st to first sc—24 sc. Cut C.
Rnd 3 Join D with sl st in any sc, ch 2, 2 hdc in same st with sl st, *ch 1, skip 1 sc, 2 hdc in next sc, ch 2, skip 1 sc, 2 hdc in next sc; rep from * 4 times more, ch 1, skip next sc, 2 hdc in 1 sc, ch 2, join to first hdc. Cut D.
Rnd 4 Join B with sl st in any ch-2 space, ch 1 (1 sc, ch 2, 1 sc), in same space as sl st, *1 sc in each of next 2 hdc, 1 sc in next ch-1 space, 1 sc in each of next 2 hdc, (1 sc, ch 2, 1 sc) in next ch-2 space; rep from * 4 times more, end 1 sc in each of next 2 hdc, 1 sc in next ch-1 space, 1 sc in each of next 2 hdc. Join and fasten off.
Motif 4 (make 4)
Work as for motif 3, only work rnd 1 with B, rnd 2 with D, rnd 3 with A and rnd 4 with B.
Motif 5 (make 2)
With C, ch 3, join with sl st to form ring.
Rnd 1 Ch 1, work 5 sc in ring, join and fasten off C.
Rnd 2 Join A with sl st in any sc, ch 2, (yo and draw up a loop) twice in same sc, yo and draw through all loops on hook and ch 1 (for beg cluster), ch 2, (yo and draw up a loop) 3 times in same sc as beg cluster, yo and through all loops on hook and ch 1 (for cluster), *(work cluster, ch 2, cluster) in next sc; rep from * 3 times more, join. Cut A.
Rnd 3 Join D with sl st in any ch-2 space, ch 1 (1 sc, ch 2, 1 sc) in same space, *3 sc between next 2 clusters, (1 sc, ch 2, 1 sc) in next ch-2 space; rep from * 3 times more, end 3 sc between next 2 clusters, join. Cut D.

Rnd 4 Join A with sl st in any ch-2 space, ch 1, (1 sc, ch 2, 1 sc) in same space, *1 sc in each of next 5 sc, (1 sc, ch 2, 1 sc) in next ch-2 space; rep from * 3 times more, end 1 sc in each of last 5 sc. Join and fasten off.

Motif 6 (make 2)

Work as for motif 5, only work rnd 1 with B, rnd 2 with D, rnd 3 with C and rnd 4 with D.

Motif 7 (make 2)

With A, ch 3, join with sl st to form ring.

Rnd 1 Ch 2, work 10 hdc in ring, join to first hdc. Cut A.

Rnd 2 Join C with sl st to any hdc, ch 1, 2 sc in same st with sl st, 2 sc in each of next 9 hdc, join D with sl st to first sc—20 sc. Cut C.

Rnd 3 Join D with sl st in any sc, ch 2, 2 hdc in same st with sl st, *ch 1, skip 1 sc, 2 hdc in next sc, ch 2, skip 1 sc, 2 hdc in next sc; rep from * 3 times more, ch 1, skip next sc, 2 hdc in next sc, ch 2, join to first hdc. Cut D.

Rnd 4 Join B with sl st in any ch-2 space, ch 1, (1 sc, ch 2, 1 sc) in same space as sl st, *1 sc in each of next 2 hdc, 1 sc in next ch-1 space, 1 sc in each of next 2 hdc, (1 sc, ch 2, 1 sc) in next ch-2 space; rep from * 3 times more, end 1 sc in each of next 2 hdc, 1 sc in next ch-1 space, 1 sc in each of next 2 hdc. Join and fasten off.

Motif 8 (make 2)

Work as for motif 7, only work rnd 1 with B, rnd 2 with D, rnd 3 with A and rnd 4 with B.

Joining Motifs

Hat is composed of 3 sets of joined strips (with 8 motifs in each strip) and a center top motif. Use D to sl st the motifs tog on WS along one edge only.

First strip

For the lower edge strip (alternate motifs 1 or 2 with motifs 3 or 4) 4 times.

Second strip

For the center strip, work as for first strip, alternating colors as before.

Third strip

For the top (crown strip), alternate motifs 5, 6, 7 and 8 randomly foll photo. Be sure to have 2 sides of each pentagon free on one side of the strip and one side of each pentagon free on opposite side of strip.

Top Motif

Use rem motif 3 for top of hat and join all strips tog to form hat.

Lower Edge

Rnd 1 Join B with sl st in any ch-2 space, *1 sc in each of next 2 sc, 1 hdc in each of next 2 sc, 1 dc in each of next 2 sc, yo hook twice and draw up a loop in next sc, (yo and through 2 loops) twice, yo hook twice and draw up a loop in next ch-2 space, (yo and through 2 loops) twice, yo hook twice and draw up a loop in next ch-2 space of next motif, (yo and through 2 loops) twice, yo hook twice, and draw up a loop in next sc, (yo and draw through 2 loops) twice, yo and draw through all 5 loops—Tr4tog made, 1 dc in each of next 2 sc, 1 hdc in each of next 2 sc, 1 sc in each of next 2 sc, sl st in ch-2 space; rep from * around join to first sc. Cut B.

Rnd 2 Join D with sl st in last sl st, ch 1, 1 sl in same space as sl st, *ch 1, skip 1 st, 1 sc in next st; rep from * to last st, ch 1, skip last st, join to to first sc. Cut D.

Rnd 3 Join A in any sc, ch 1, 1 sc in first sc, * 1 sc in next st located 1 row below next ch-1 space, 1 sc in next sc; rep from * to last ch-1 space, 1 sc in next st 1 row below as before, join with sl st to first sc.

Rnd 4 With A, working from left to right, work 1 reverse sc in each sc around. Fasten off.

Radius Pictures

PATRIOTIC BAG

TOOLKIT

YARN (4)
- 5¼oz/150g, 300yd/270m of any worsted weight wool in dark blue (A)
- 3½oz/100g, 200yd/180m in cream (B), light blue (C), and hot pink (D)

HOOK
- Size H/8 (5mm) crochet hook *or size to obtain gauge*

OTHER
- One 7½"/19cm wide x 6"/15cm high bamboo handle with gold handle clips
- One 12"/30.5cm matching zipper
- ½ yd/.5m of lining fabric
- Matching thread

Finished Measurements
Approx 12½"/31.5cm wide x 17"/43cm high (excluding handle).

Gauge
One square = 4¼"/10.5cm.
Take time to check gauge.

Note
All rnds are worked on the RS.

Stitch Glossary
dc2tog [Yo, insert hook into next st and draw up a lp, yo and draw through 2 lps on hook] twice, yo and draw through all 3 lps on hook.
dc3tog [Yo, insert hook into next st and draw up a lp, yo and draw through 2 lps on hook] 3 times, yo and draw through all 4 lps on hook.

Basic Granny Square
With first color, ch 4. Join ch with a sl st, forming a ring.
Rnd 1 (RS) Ch 3 (counts as 1 dc), work 2 dc in ring, [ch 3, work 3 dc in ring] 3 times, ch 3, join rnd with a sl st in 3rd ch of beg ch-3. Fasten off.
Rnd 2 Join 2nd color with a sl st in any corner ch-3 sp, ch 3 (counts as 1 dc), work (2 dc, ch 3, 3 dc) in same ch-3 sp, *ch 1, work (3 dc, ch 3, 3 dc) in next corner ch-3 sp; rep from * twice more, ch 1, join rnd with a sl st in 3rd ch of beg ch-3. Fasten off.
Rnd 3 Join 3rd color with a sl st in any corner ch-3 sp, ch 3 (counts as 1 dc), work (2 dc, ch 3, 3 dc) in same ch-3 sp, *ch 1, work 3 dc in next ch-1 sp, ch 1, work (3 dc, ch 3, 3 dc) in next corner ch-3 sp; rep from * twice more, ch 1, work 3 dc in last ch-1 sp, join rnd with a sl st in 3rd ch of beg ch-3. Fasten off.
Rnd 4 Join 4th color with a sl st in any corner ch-3 sp, ch 3 (counts as 1 dc), work (2 dc, ch 3, 3 dc) in same ch-3 sp, *[ch 1, work 3 dc in next ch-1 sp] twice, ch 1, work (3 dc, ch 3, 3 dc) in next corner ch-3 sp; rep from * twice more, [ch 1, work 3 dc in last ch-1 sp] twice, join rnd with a sl st in 3rd ch of beg ch-3. Fasten off.
Make 14 squares (7 for front and 7 for back) foll diagram for colorways.

Bottom Corner Square (make 4)
With B, ch 4. Join ch with a sl st, forming a ring.
Rnd 1 (RS) Rep rnd 1 as for basic square.
Rnd 2 With D, rep rnd 2 as for basic square.
Rnd 3 Join C with a sl st in any corner ch-3 sp, ch 3 (counts as 1 dc), work (2 dc, ch 3, 3 dc) in same ch-3 sp, ch 1, work 3 dc in next ch-1 sp, ch 1, *work (3 dc, ch 3, 3 dc) in next corner ch-3 sp, ch 1, work 3 dc in next ch-1 sp*, ch 3, work 3 sc in next ch-3 sp, ch 3, work 3 dc in next ch-1 sp, ch 1, rep from * to * once more, ch 1, join with sl st in 3rd ch of beg ch-3. Fasten off.
Rnd 4 Join A with a sl st in corner ch-3 sp opposite corner where 3 sc were worked, ch 3 (counts as 1 dc), work (2 dc, ch 3, 3 dc) in same ch-3 sp, [ch 1, work 3 dc in next ch-1 sp] twice, ch 1, work (3 dc, ch 3, 3 dc) in next corner ch-3 sp, ch 1, work 3 dc in next ch-1 sp,

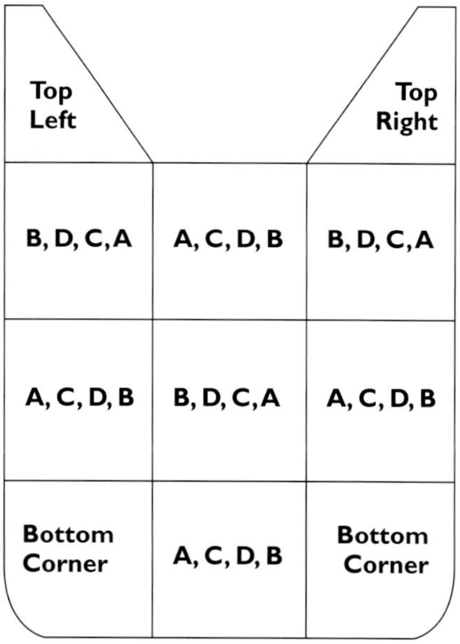

FRONT & BACK

ch 1, work 3 sc in next ch-3 sp, sc in next sc, work 3 sc in next sc, sc in next sc, work 3 sc in next ch-3 sp, ch 1, work 3 dc in next ch-1 sp, ch 1, work (3 dc, ch 3, 3 dc) in next corner ch-3 sp, [ch 1, work 3 dc in next ch-1 sp] twice, ch 1, join rnd with a sl st in 3rd ch of beg ch-3. Fasten off.

Right Top Corner Half-Square

(make 2)

With A, ch 4. Join ch with a sl st, forming a ring.

Rnd 1 (RS) Rep rnd 1 as for basic square.

Rnd 2 Join C with a sl st in any corner ch-3 sp, ch 3 (counts as 1 dc), work (2 dc, ch 3, 3 dc) in same ch-3 sp, ch 3, sc in next ch-3 sp, ch 3, [work (3 dc, ch 3, 3 dc) in next corner ch-3 sp, ch 1] twice (placing a yarn marker in first ch-3 sp worked), join rnd with a sl st in 3rd ch of beg ch-3. Fasten off.

Row 3 Join D with a sl st in marked corner ch-3 sp, ch 3 (counts as 1 dc), work 3 dc in same ch-3 sp, ch 1, work 3 dc in next ch-1 sp, ch 1, work (3 dc, ch 3, 3 dc) in next corner ch-3 sp, ch 1, work 3 dc in next ch-1 sp, ch 1, work 4 dc in next corner ch-3 sp. Fasten off, leaving rem sts unworked.

Row 4 Join B with a sl st in 3rd ch of beg ch-3 of row 3, ch 3 (counts as 1 dc), work 3 dc in same sp, [ch 1, work 3 dc in next ch-1 sp] twice, ch 1, work (3 dc, ch 3, 3 dc) in next corner ch-3 sp, [ch 1, work 3 dc in next ch-1 sp] twice, ch 3, sc in top of last dc of row 3, ch 3, work 2 dc in side edge of same dc of row 3, dc in ch-3 corner sp of rnd 2, dc in next 3 dc of rnd 2, dc in next ch-3 sp. Ch 3, turn.

Row 5 [Dc2tog] 3 times, dc in top of ch 3 of row 4—4 sts. Ch 3, turn.

Row 6 Dc3tog, dc in top of ch 3. Fasten off.

Left Top Corner Half-Square

(make 2)

Work as for right top corner half-square until row 3 is completed.

Row 4 (RS) Join B with a sl st in top of beg ch-3 of row 3, ch 3, dc in next 3 dc of rnd 2, dc in ch-3 corner sp of rnd 2, work 2 dc in side edge of dc of row 3, ch 3, sc in top of first dc of row 3, ch 3, [work 3 dc in next ch-1 sp, ch 1] twice, work (3 dc, ch 3, 3 dc) in next corner ch-3 sp, [ch 1, work 3 dc in net ch-1 sp] twice, ch 1, work 4 dc in last dc. Fasten off.

Row 5 With RS facing, join B with a sl st in 3rd ch of beg ch-3 of row 4, ch 3, [dc2tog] 3 times—4 sts. Ch 3, turn.

Row 6 Dc3tog, dc in top of ch 3. Fasten off.

Finishing

Using A, sc squares tog foll placement diagram, joining squares across first to form strips, then join strips together to form front (or back) of bag.

Lining

Fold lining fabric in half, RS facing. Trace front onto lining fabric. Cut out pieces ½"/1.3cm larger all around. Using a ½"/1.3cm seam allowance, sew

Jack Deutsch Studio

side and bottom seams. Trim seams to ¼"/.5cm. Make ½"/1.3cm deep clips along curved edges of top. Turn top edge ½"/1.3cm to WS and press. Set aside.

Edging

With RS facing, join A with a sl st in top right corner of bag back. **Row 1** Ch 1, making sure that work lies flat, sc evenly along entire edge. Fasten off. Rep for bag front. To sc front and back tog, place pieces tog, WS facing. Working through both thicknesses, join A with a sl st in left top corner. **Row 2** Ch 1, making sure that work lies flat, sc evenly across side and bottom edges, working 3 sc in each bottom corner. Fasten off. Sew in zipper. Insert lining. Sew top edges of lining in place, having pressed edge approx ⅛"/.3cm from zipper teeth. Using A, whipstitch handle clips to each top corner.

PRETTY POSIES SKIRT

Sizes
Instructions are written for size Small/ Medium.

Finished Measurements
Lower edge 56"/142cm.
Waist 36"/91.5cm.
Length 25"/63.5cm.

Gauges
Large motif = 3½"/9cm using larger crochet hook.
Small motif = 3"/7.5cm using smaller crochet hook.
Take time to check gauges.

Notes
1 To join yarn with a sc, make a slipknot and place on hook. Insert hook in st, yo, draw up a lp, yo and draw through both lps on hook.
2 Skirt is made of 7 horizontal strips of 16 motifs each. Referring to diagram and following it from left to right, work the 4-motif rep 4 times across for each strip.
3 Use larger hook to make strips 1–4 for bottom of skirt, then use smaller hook to rep strips 1–3 for top of skirt.

TOOLKIT

YARN (4)
- *Wool Ease* by Lion Brand Yarn Co., 3oz/85g, 200yd/180m, wool and acrylic blend
  3 skeins each in #188 Paprika and #126 Chocolate brown
- 1 skein each in #129 Cocoa and #174 Avocado

HOOKS
- Size H/8 and I/9 (5 and 5.5mm) crochet hooks *or sizes to obtain gauges*

Stitch Glossary
CL (cluster st) In same sp [yo, insert hook into ring, yo and draw up a lp, yo and draw through 2 lps on hook] 3 times, yo and draw through all 4 lps on hook.
dc2tog In same sp [yo, insert hook into ring, yo and draw up a lp, yo and draw through 2 lps on hook] twice, yo and draw through all 3 lps on hook.

Skirt
First motif
With larger hook and paprika, ch 6. Join ch with a sl st forming a ring.
Rnd 1 (RS) Ch 3 (counts as 1 dc), dc2tog in ring (beg CL made), ch 3, [CL in ring, ch 3] 7 times, join rnd with a sl st in top of beg CL—8 CL sts. Fasten off.
Rnd 2 (RS) Join chocolate brown with a sc in top of any CL st, ch 3, CL in next ch-3 sp, ch 3, [sc in top of next CL, ch 3, CL in next ch-3 sp, ch 3] 7 times, join rnd with a sl st in first sc. Fasten off.

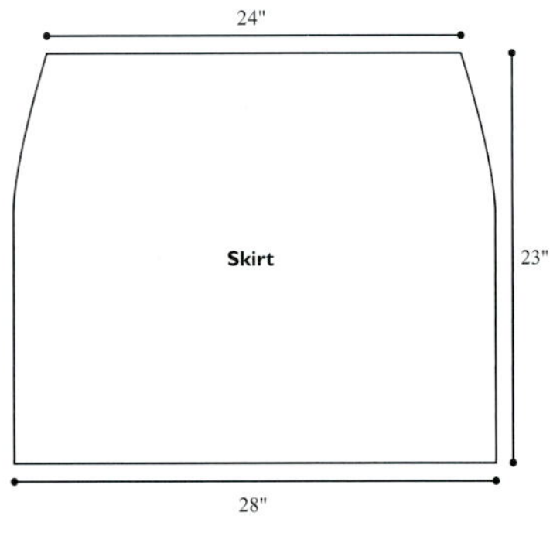

Expert hint:

Subtle A-line shaping is created by using two different sized crochet hooks—a larger hook flares out the bottom, while a smaller one shapes the top .

Jack Deutsch Studio

Making and Joining Second Motif
With larger hook and cocoa, ch 6. Join ch with a sl st, forming a ring.
Rnd 1 (RS) Rep rnd 1 as for first motif.
Rnd 2 (joining) With RS facing, join chocolate brown with a sc in top of any CL st, ch 3, CL in next ch-3 sp, ch 3, sc in top of next CL, ch 3, CL in next ch-3 sp, sl st in corresponding CL of first motif, ch 3, sc in top of next CL of 2nd motif, ch 3, CL in next ch-3 sp of 2nd motif, sl st in corresponding CL of first motif, ch 3, cont around 2nd motif as foll: [sc in top of next CL, ch 3, CL in next ch-3 sp, ch3] 5 times, join rnd with a sl st in first sc. Fasten off.
Making and Joining Next 14 Motifs
Cont to join motifs as for 2nd motif until 15 motifs are joined. Make and join the 16th motif to the 15th motif and then the first motif, forming a circle.
Making and Joining Rem Motifs
Cont to work in the same manner, joining motifs on rnd 2 to each corresponding CL st with a sl st and joining last 2 motifs to cont the circle.
Filler Motifs
Use larger hook for bottom 4 strips and smaller hook for top 3 strips.
With paprika, ch 4. Join ch with a sl st, forming a ring.
Rnd 1 (RS) *Ch 3, sl st in matching sc of adjoining motif, ch 3, sc in ring; rep from * 3 times more. Fasten off.

Finishing

Lightly block to measurements.
Waistband
Rnd 1 (RS) With smaller hook, join paprika with sl st in sc between top 2 clusters of any square at top edge, ch 5 (counts 1 hdc and ch 3), *sc in top of next CL, dc2tog in next sc of same motif, dc2tog in opposite sc of next adjoining motif, sc in top of next CL, ch 3**, hdc in next sc, ch 3; rep from * around, end last rep at **, join rnd with a sl st in 2nd ch of beg ch-5.
Rnd 2 Ch 1, sc in same space with joining, *2 sc in next ch-3 sp, sc in next sc, [sc in next dc2tog] twice, sc in next sc, 2 sc in next ch-3 sp, sc in next hdc; rep from * around, end last rep with 2 sc in last ch-3 sp, join rnd with a sl st in first sc.
Rnds 3–5 Ch 3 (counts as 1 dc), dc in each st around, join rnd with a sl st to top of beg ch-3. When rnd 5 is completed, fasten off.
Drawstring
With larger hook and 2 strands of paprika held tog, ch for 76"/193cm. Fasten off. Beg and ending at center front, weave drawstring over and under every 2 dc around. Knot ends of drawstring.

PATCHWORK SHAWL

TOOLKIT

YARN (4)
- 14oz/400g, 710yd/640m of any worsted weight wool blend in black (A)
- 7oz/200g, 360yd/320m in cream (B)
- 5¼oz/150g, 270yd/240m in red multi (C)
- 3½oz/100g, 180yd/160m in plum (D) and brown (E)
- 1¾ oz/50g, 90yd/80m in purple (F) cranberry (G)

HOOK
- Size G/7 (4.5mm) crochet hook or *size to obtain gauge*

Finished Measurements
Approx 79"/200cm wide along top of triangle and 43"/109cm deep.

Gauge
Square A = 5½"/14cm, including black edge.
Take time to check gauge.

Square A
Make a total of 22 in colors as described later.
Ch 4, join with sl st to form ring.
Rnd 1 [Work 1 sc in ring, ch 3] 4 times, join with sl st to first sc.
Rnd 2 Sl st in ch-3 sp, ch 3 (counts as 1 dc), 2 dc, ch 3 and 3 dc in same sp for corner, *3 dc, ch 3 and 3 dc in next sp; rep from * twice, join with sl st to top of ch-3. Fasten off.
Rnd 3 With loop on hook, 1 sc in a corner ch-2 sp, ch 3, 1 sc in same sp, *ch 3, 1 sc between next 3rd and 4th dc's, ch 3, 1 sc, ch 3 and 1 sc in corner; rep from *, end ch 3, join with sl st to first sc.
Rnd 4 Sl st in corner ch-3 sp, ch 3 (counts as 1 dc), 2 dc, ch 3 and 3 dc in corner, *3 dc in each ch-3 sp to next corner, 3 dc, ch 3 and 3 dc in corner; rep from *, end 3 dc in last sp, join to top of first ch-3. Fasten off.
Rnd 5 With loop on hook, 1 sc in corner sp, ch 3, 1 sc in same sp, *ch 3, 1 sc between each of the next 3rd and 4th dc's to next corner, 1 sc, ch 3 and 1 sc in corner; rep from *, end ch 3, join with sl st to first sc.
Rnd 6 Rep rnd 4.
Rnd 7 With black (A) on all squares, *work sc in one sp between 3 dc group, ch 5; rep from * to corner, work sc, ch 7 and sc in corner, ch 5; rep from * around. Join to first sc. Fasten off.

Square B
Make a total of 6 in colors as described later.
Ch 6, join with sl st to form ring.
Rnd 1 Ch 3 (counts as 1 dc), work 15 dc in ring, join with sl st first dc. Fasten off.
Rnd 2 With loop on hook, work 1 dc in any dc, ch 2, *1 dc in next dc, ch 2; rep from * around—16 dc and ch-2 sps. Join with sl st to top of first dc. Fasten off.
Rnd 3 With loop on hook, work 2 dc in any ch-2 sp for start of corner, *ch 1, [2 dc in next sp, ch 1] 4 times, ch 3 for corner, 2 dc in same corner sp; rep from * ending ch 1, [2 dc in next sp, ch 1] 4 times, ch 3 for corner, join with sl st to top of dc. Fasten off.
Rnd 4 With loop on hook, 1 sc in corner ch-3 sp, ch 3, 1 sc in same sp, *ch 3, 1 sc in 2nd dc of 2 dc group; rep from * twice, ch 3, 1 sc, ch 3 and 1 sc in corner; rep from * around, end ch 3, join with sl st to top of first sc. Fasten off.
Rnd 5 Work rnd 4 of square A.
Rnd 6 Work rnd 7 of square A.

Triangle C
Make a total of 8 in colors as described later. Ch 4, join with sl st to form ring.
Row 1 [Work 1 sc in ring, ch 3] 3 times, 1 sc in ring, turn.
Row 2 Ch 3 (counts as 1 dc), 3 dc in ch 3-sp, 3 dc, ch 3 and 3 dc in corner sp, 3 dc in last sp, Fasten off. Turn.
Row 3 With loop on hook, sc in top of first dc, ch 3, sc in same st, [ch 3, sc between next 3rd and 4th dc's] twice, ch 3, sc in same corner sp, [ch 3, sc between next 3rd and 4th dc's] twice, ch 3, sc in same sp as last sc, turn.
Row 4 Ch 3 (counts as 1 dc), 2 dc in first ch-3 sp, 3 dc in each ch-3 sp to corner, 3 dc, ch 3 and 3 dc in corner, 3 dc in each ch-3 sp to end. Fasten off. Turn.
Row 5 With loop on hook, sc in top of first dc, ch 3, sc in same st, *ch 3, sc between next 3rd and 4th dc's to corner, ch 3, sc, ch 3, sc in corner sp; rep

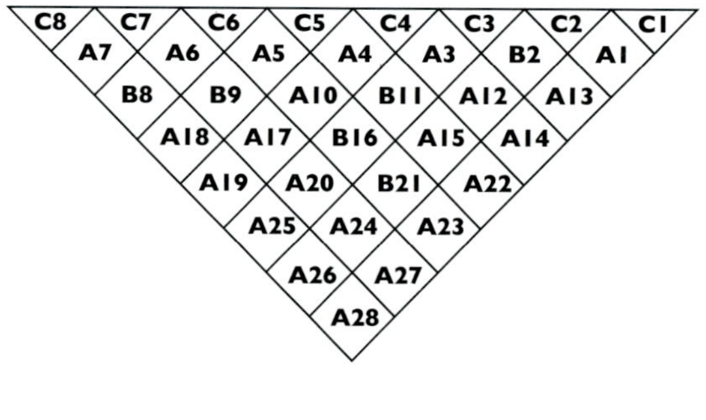

Brian Kraus, NYC (Butterick)

from *, end ch 3, sc in same dc as last sc. Turn.
Row 6 Rep row 4.
Row 7 With black (A), work sc in first dc, ch 7, sc in same dc, *ch 5, sc between 3rd and 4th dc's; rep from * to corner, ch 7, sc in corner, rep from * to end. Fasten off.

Color Sequence

Note All final rnds are worked with black (A) foll instructions for squares.

Square A1
Beg with plum (D), work rnds 1 and 2 with D, rnd 3 with cream (B), rnd 4 with plum (D), rnd 5 with cream (B), rnd 6 with purple (F).
Square B2
Beg with black (A), work rnd 1 with A, rnd 2 with cream (B), rnd 3 with cranberry (G), rnd 4 with cream (B), rnd 5 with brown (E).
Square A3
Beg with brown (E), work rnds 1 and 2 with E, rnds 3 and 4 with cream (B), rnds 5 and 6 with plum (D).
Square A4
Beg with cranberry (G), work rnds 1-4 with G, rnd 5 with purple (F), rnd 6 with cranberry (G).
Square A5
Beg with purple (F), work rnds 1 and 2 with F, rnds 3 and 4 with plum (D), rnds 5 and 6 with purple (F).
Square A6
Beg with plum (D), work rnd 1 with D, rnd 2 with brown (E), rnd 3 with D, rnd 4 with E, rnd 5 with D, rnd 6 with E.
Square A7
Beg with cranberry (G), work rnds 1-4 with G, rnd 5 with cream (B), rnd 6 with purple (F).
Square B8
Beg with plum (D), work rnd 1 with D, rnd 2 with purple (F), rnd 3 with cream (B), rnd 4 with plum (D), rnd 5 with cream (B).
Square B9
Beg with cream (B), work rnd 1 with B, rnd 2 with black (A), rnd 3 with red multi (C), rnd 4 with chestnut (E), rnd 5 with cranberry (G).
Square A10
Beg with black (A), work rnds 1 and 2 with A, rnd 3 with chestnut (E), rnd 4 with cranberry (G), rnd 5 with cream (B), rnd 6 with red multi (C).
Square B11
Beg with red multi (C), work rnd 1 with C, rnd 2 with brown (E), rnd 3 with C, rnds 4 and 5 with E.
Square A12
Beg with brown (E), work rnds 1 and 2 with E, rnd 3 with cream (B), rnd 4 with E, rnd 5 with B, rnd 6 with plum (D).
Square A13
Beg with cream (B), work rnds 1 and 2 with B, rnds 3 and 4 with cranberry (G), rnds 5 and 6 with red multi (C).
Square A14
Beg with black (A), work rnd 1 with A, rnds 2-4 with red multi (C), rnd 5 with A, rnd 6 with plum (D).
Square A15
Beg with black (A), work rnd 1 with A, rnd 2 with plum (D), rnds 3 and 4 with cream (B), rnd 5 with cranberry (G), rnd 6 with B.
Square B16
Beg with cranberry (G), work rnd 1 with G, rnd 2 with cream (B), rnd 3 with purple (F), rnds 4 and 5 with red multi (C).
Square A17
Beg with cream (B), work rnd 1 with B, rnd 2 with brown (E), rnds 3 and 4 with plum (D), rnd 5 with black (A), rnd 6 with cream (B).
Square A18
Beg with red multi (C), work rnd 1 with C, rnd 2 with purple (F), rnds 3 and 4 with cranberry (G), rnd 5 with brown (E), rnd 6 with G.
Square A19
Beg with red multi (C), work rnd 1 with C, rnd 2

with cream (B), rnds 3 and 4 with C, rnd 5 with B, rnd 6 with C.

Square A20

Beg with brown (E), work rnd 1 with E, rnd 2 with purple (F), rnds 3 and 4 with plum (D), rnd 5 with brown (E), rnd 6 with purple (F).

Square B21

Beg with cream (B), work rnd 1 with B, rnd 2 with brown (E), rnd 3 with plum (D), rnds 4 and 5 with cranberry (G).

Square A22

Beg with brown (E), work rnd 1 with E, rnd 2 with black (A), rnd 3 with E, rnd 4 with cranberry (G), rnd 5 with purple (F), rnd 6 with plum (D).

Square A23

Beg with black (A), work rnds 1 and 2 with A, rnd 3 with purple (F), rnd 4 with plum (D), rnd 5 with cream (B), rnd 6 with red multi (C).

Square A24

Beg with red multi (C), work rnd 1 with C, rnd 2 with plum (D), rnd 3 with C, rnd 4 with D, rnd 5 with C, rnd 6 with D.

Square A25

Beg with plum (D), work rnds 1 and 2 with D, rnds 3 and 4 with red multi (C), rnd 5 with purple (F), rnd 6 with brown (E).

Square A26

Beg with cream (B), work rnd 1 with B, rnd 2 with red multi (C), rnds 3 and 4 with B, rnd 5 with black (A), rnd 6 with plum (D).

Square A27

Beg with red multi (C), work rnds 1 and 2 with C, rnds 3 and 4 with black (A), rnds 5 and 6 with C.

Square A28

Beg with brown (E), work rnds 1 and 2 with E, rnds 3 and 4 with cranberry (G), rnd 5 with black (A), rnd 6 with cream (B).

Triangle C1

Beg with cream (B), work rows 1 and 2 with B, rows 3 and 4 with red multi (C), row 5 with B, row 6 with cranberry (G).

Triangle C2

Beg with black (A), work row 1 with A, row 2 with red multi (C), row 3 with A, row 4 with brown (E), row 5 with purple (F), row 6 with E.

Triangle C3

Beg with cranberry (G), work rows 1 and 2 with G, row 3 with purple (F), row 4 with brown (E), row 5 with F, row 6 with G.

Triangle C4

Beg with black (A), work rows 1 and 2 with A, row 3 with red multi (C), row 4 with brown (E), row 5 with C, row 6 with plum (D).

Triangle C5

Beg with plum (D), work rows 1 and 2 with D, row 3 with cream (B), row 4 with brown (E), row 5 with B, row 6 with cranberry (G).

Triangle C6

Beg with red multi (C), work rows 1 and 2 with C, row 3 with black (A), row 4 with cream (B), row 5 with A, row 6 with C.

Triangle C7

Beg with purple (F), work rows 1 and 2 with F, row 3 with plum (D), row 4 with F, row 5 with D, row 6 with F.

Triangle C8

Beg with brown (E), work rows 1 and 2 with E, row 3 with plum (D), row 4 with E, rows 5 and 6 with red multi (C).

Finishing

Lay out motifs foll diagram.

Join Squares

To join squares, using black (A), *sc in corner lp of one square, ch 2, sc in corresponding lp of adjoining square; rep from * until sides of square are joined. To join squares at center point of 4 squares, work a ch-2 joining to 2 diagonally opposite squares, then a ch-3 joining with 2nd ch worked through the center of this joining.

TRICOLOR SQUARE SKIRT

TOOLKIT

YARN (4)
- 3½oz/100g, 210yd/190m of any worsted weight wool in teal (A), blue (B), and light blue (C)

HOOK
- Size H/8 (5mm) crochet hook *or size to obtain gauge*

OTHER
- 1"/2.5cm elastic to fit waistband
- Stitch markers

Sizes
Sized for X-Small/Small, Medium/Large. Shown in size Small.

Finished Measurements
Waist 30 (36)"/76 (91.5)cm.
Hips 34 (40)"/ 86.5 (101.5)cm.
Length 18½ (21½)"/47 (54.5)cm.

Gauge
Rnds 1–4 in granny square pat = 4½"/11cm.
Take time to check gauge.

Granny Square
(make 2 pieces)
With A, ch 7, join with sl st in first ch to form ring.
Rnd 1 Ch 4 (counts as 1 dc, ch 1), [1 dc into ring, ch 1] 11 times, join with sl st to 3rd ch of beg ch 4—12 ch-1 spaces. Fasten off.
Rnd 2 With B, join to any ch-1 sp, ch 5 (counts as 1 dc, ch 2), *[2 dc in next ch-1 sp, ch 1] twice, 2 dc in next ch-1 sp, ch 2; rep from * twice more, [2 dc in next ch-1 sp, ch 1] twice, 1 dc in same ch-1 sp as beg ch-5, join with sl st to 3rd ch of beg ch-5. Fasten off.
Rnd 3 With C, join to any ch-2 sp, ch 3, (2 dc, ch 2, 3 dc) in same ch-2 sp, ch 1 *[1 dc in next ch-1 sp, ch 1] twice, (3 dc, ch 2, 3 dc) in next ch-2 sp, ch 1; rep from* twice more, [1 dc in next ch-1 sp, ch 1] twice, join with sl st to 3rd ch of beg ch. Fasten off.
Rnd 4 With A, join to any ch-2 sp, ch 3, (2 dc, ch 2, 3 dc) in same ch-2 sp, ch 1, [2 dc in next ch-1 sp, ch 1, 1 dc in next ch-1 sp, ch 1, 2 dc in next ch-1 sp, ch 1, (3 dc, ch 2, 3 dc) in next ch-2 sp, ch 1] 3 times, 2 dc in next ch-1 sp, ch 1, 1 dc in next ch-1 sp, ch 1, 2 dc in next ch-1 sp, ch 1, join with sl st to 3rd ch of beg ch. Fasten off.
Rnd 5 With B, join to any ch-2 sp, ch 3, (2 dc, ch 2, 3 dc) in same ch-2 sp, ch 1, *2 dc in next ch-1 sp, ch 1, [1 dc in next ch-1 sp, ch-1] twice, 2 dc in next ch-1 sp, ch 1, (3 dc, ch 2, 3 dc) in next ch-2 sp, ch 1; rep from * twice more, 2 dc in next ch-1 sp, ch 1, [1 dc in next ch-1 sp, ch 1] twice, 2 dc in next ch-1 sp, ch 1, join with sl st to 3rd ch of beg ch. Fasten off.

Paul Amato for Lvarepresents

Rnd 6 With C, join to any ch-2 sp, ch 3, (2 dc, ch 2, 3 dc) in same ch-2 sp, ch 1, *[2 dc in next ch-1 sp, ch 1] twice, 1 dc in next ch-1 sp, ch 1, [2 dc in next ch-1 sp, ch 1] twice, (3 dc, ch 2, 3 dc) in next ch-2 sp, ch 1; rep from * twice more, [2 dc in next ch-1 sp, ch 1] twice, 1 dc in next ch-1 sp, ch 1, [2 dc in next ch-1 sp, ch 1] twice, join with sl st to 3rd ch of beg ch. Fasten off.
Rnd 7 With A, join to any ch-2 sp, ch 3, (2 dc, ch 2, 3 dc) in same ch-2 sp, ch 1, *[2 dc in next ch-1 sp, ch 1] twice, [1 dc in next ch-1 sp, ch 1] twice, [2 dc in next ch-1 sp, ch 1] twice, (3 dc, ch 2, 3 dc) in next ch-2 sp, ch 1; rep from * twice more, [2 dc in next ch-1 sp, ch 1] twice, [1 dc in next ch-1 sp, ch 1] twice, [2 dc in next ch-1 sp, ch 1] twice, join with sl st to 3rd ch of beg ch. Fasten off.
Rnd 8 With B, join to any ch-2 sp, ch 3, (2 dc, ch 2, 3 dc) in same ch-2 sp), ch 1, *[2 dc in next ch-1 sp, ch 1] 3 times, 1 dc in next ch-1 sp, ch 1, [2 dc in next ch-1 sp, ch 1] 3 times, (3 dc, ch 2, 3 dc) in next ch-2 sp, ch 1; rep from * twice more, [2 dc in next ch-1 sp, ch 1] 3 times, 1 dc in next ch-1 sp, ch 1, [2 dc in next ch-1 sp, ch 1] 3 times, join with sl st to 3rd ch of beg ch. Fasten off.
Rnd 9 With C, join to any ch-2 sp, ch 3, (2 dc, ch 2, 3 dc) in same ch-2 sp, ch 1, *[2 dc in next ch-1 sp, ch 1] 3 times, [1 dc in next ch-1 sp, ch 1] twice, [2 dc in next ch-1 sp, ch 1] 3 times, (3 dc, ch 2, 3 dc) in next ch-2 sp, ch 1; rep from * twice more, [2 dc in next ch-1 sp, ch 1] 3 times, [1 dc in next ch-1 sp, ch 1] twice, [2 dc in next ch-1 sp, ch 1] 3 times, join with sl st to 3rd ch of beg ch. Fasten off.
Rnd 10 With A, join to any ch-2 sp, ch 3, (2 dc, ch 2, 3 dc) in same ch-2 sp, ch 1, *[2 dc in next ch-1 sp, ch 1] 4 times, 1 dc in next ch-1 sp, ch 1, [2 dc in next ch-1 sp, ch 1] 4 times, (3 dc, ch 2, 3 dc) in next ch-2 sp, ch 1; rep from * twice more, [2 dc in next ch-1 sp, ch 1] 4 times, 1 dc in next ch-1 sp, ch 1, [2 dc in next ch-1 sp, ch 1] 4 times, join with sl st to 3rd ch of beg ch. Fasten off.
Rnd 11 With B, join to any ch-2 sp, ch 3, (2 dc, ch 2, 3 dc) in same ch-2 sp, ch 1, *[2 dc in next ch-1 sp, ch 1] 4 times, [1 dc in next ch-1 sp, ch 1] twice, [2 dc in next ch-1 sp, ch 1] 4 times, (3 dc, ch 2, 3 dc) in next ch-2 sp, ch 1; rep from * twice more, [2 dc in next ch-1 sp, ch 1] 4 times, [1 dc in next ch-1 sp, ch 1] twice, [2 dc in next ch-1 sp, ch 1] 4 times, join with sl st to 3rd ch of beg ch. Fasten off.
Rnd 12 With C, join to any ch-2 sp, ch 3, (2 dc, ch 2, 3 dc) in same ch-2 sp, ch 1, *[2 dc in next ch-1 sp, ch 1] 5 times, 1 dc in next ch 1 sp, ch 1, [2 dc in next ch-1 sp, ch 1] 5 times, (3 dc, ch 2, 3 dc) in next ch-2 sp, ch 1; rep from * twice more, [2 dc in next ch-1 sp, ch 1] 5 times, 1 dc in next ch-1 sp, ch 1, [2 dc in next ch-1 sp, ch 1] 5 times, join with sl st to 3rd ch of beg ch. Fasten off.

Rnd 13 With A, join to any ch-2 sp, ch 3, (2 dc, ch 2, 3 dc) in same ch-2 sp, ch 1, *[2 dc in next ch-1 sp, ch 1] 5 times, [1 dc in next ch-1 sp, ch 1] twice, [2 dc in next ch-1 sp, ch 1] 5 times, (3 dc, ch 2, 3 dc) in next ch-2 sp, ch 1; rep from * twice more, [2 dc in next ch-1 sp, ch 1] 5 times, [1 dc in next ch-1 sp, ch 1] twice, [2 dc in next ch-1 sp, ch 1] 5 times, join with sl st to 3rd ch of beg ch. Fasten off.

Rnd 14 With B, join to any ch-2 sp, ch 3, (2 dc, ch 2, 3 dc) in same ch-2 sp, ch 1, *[2 dc in next ch-1 sp, ch 1] 6 times, 1 dc in next ch-1 sp, ch 1, [2 dc in next ch-1 sp, ch 1] 6 times, (3 dc, ch 2, 3 dc) in next ch-2 sp, ch 1; rep from * twice more, [2 dc in next ch-1 sp, ch 1] 6 times, 1 dc in next ch-1 sp, ch 1, [2 dc in next ch-1 sp, ch 1] 6 times, join with sl st to 3rd ch of beg ch. Fasten off.

Rnd 15 With C, join to any ch-2 sp, ch 3, (2 dc, ch 2, 3 dc) in same ch-2 sp, ch 1, *[2 dc in next ch-1 sp, ch 1] 6 times, [1 dc in next ch-1 sp, ch 1] twice, [2 dc in next ch-1 sp, ch 1] 6 times, (3 dc, ch 2, 3 dc) in next ch-2 sp, ch 1; rep from * twice more, [2 dc in next ch-1 sp, ch 1] 6 times, [1 dc in next ch-1 sp, ch 1] twice, [2 dc in next ch-1 sp, ch 1] 6 times, join with sl st to 3rd ch of beg ch. Fasten off.

For Medium/Large Size Only

Rnd 16 With A, join to any ch-2 sp, ch 3, (2 dc, ch 2, 3 dc) in same ch-2 sp, ch 1, *[2 dc in next ch-1 sp, ch 1] 7 times, 1 dc in next ch 1 sp, ch 1, [2 dc in next ch-1 sp, ch 1] 7 times, (3 dc, ch 2, 3 dc) in next ch-2 sp, ch 1; rep from * twice more, [2 dc in next ch-1 sp, ch 1] 7 times, 1 dc in next ch-1 sp, ch 1, [2 dc in next ch-1 sp, ch 1] 7 times, join with sl st to 3rd ch of beg ch. Fasten off.

Rnd 17 With B, join to any ch-2 sp, ch 3, (2 dc, ch 2, 3 dc) in same ch-2 sp, ch 1, *[2 dc in next ch-1 sp, ch 1] 7 times, [1 dc in next ch-1 sp, ch 1] twice, [2 dc in next ch-1 sp, ch 1] 7 times, (3 dc, ch 2, 3 dc) in next ch-2 sp, ch 1; rep from * twice more, [2 dc in next ch-1 sp, ch 1] 7 times, [1 dc in next ch-1 sp, ch 1] twice, [2 dc in next ch-1 sp, ch 1] 7 times, join with sl st to 3rd ch of beg ch. Fasten off.

Rnd 18 With C, join to any ch-2 sp, ch 3, (2 dc, ch 2, 3 dc) in same ch-2 sp, ch 1, *[2 dc in next ch-1 sp, ch 1] 8 times, 1 dc in next ch-1 sp, ch 1, [2 dc in next ch-1 sp, ch 1] 8 times, (3 dc, ch 2, 3 dc) in next ch-2 sp, ch 1; rep from * twice more, [2 dc in next ch-1 sp, ch 1] 8 times, 1 dc in next ch-1 sp, ch 1, [2 dc in next ch-1 sp, ch 1] 8 times, join with sl st to 3rd ch of beg ch. Fasten off.

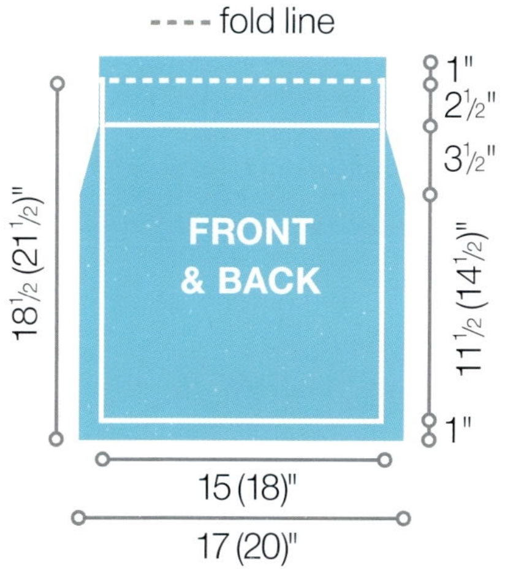

For All Sizes

Side shaping

Mark granny square for upper edge. Place markers 3½"/9cm down from upper edge on each side. **Row 1** With A and RS facing, join in 2nd ch of ch-2 space at upper edge, ch 1, 1 sc in next 3 dc, 1 hdc in next ch-1 sp, 1 hdc in each of next 2 dc, 1 hdc in next ch-1 sp, 1 dc in st to next 3-dc group, ch 1, skip 3 dc, (3 dc, ch 2, 3 dc) in ch-2 sp, ch 1, skip 3 dc, *dc in next ch-1 sp, ch 1; rep from * to next 3-dc group, skip 3 dc, (3 dc, ch 2, 3 dc) in ch-2 sp, skip 3 dc, ch 1, 1 dc in each st to marker, 1 hdc in next 4 sts, 1 sc in next 4 sts. Fasten off.

Row 2 With B, join in ch-1 of row 1, ch 1, 1 sc in next 7 sts, 1 hdc in next 4 sts, 1 dc in each st to next 3-dc group, ch 1, skip 3 dc, (3 dc, ch 2, 3 dc) in ch-2 sp, ch 1, skip 3 dc, *dc in next ch-1 sp, ch 1; rep from * to next 3-dc group, skip 3 dc, (3dc, ch 2, 3 dc) in ch-2 sp, skip 3 dc, ch 1, 1 dc in each st to marker, 1 hdc in each of next 4 sts, 1 sc in next 8 sts. Fasten off.

Finishing

Block pieces. Beg with first dc above 3-dc group, sew side seam to upper edge on each side.

Waistband

Rnd 1 Join A to side seam with sl st , ch 3 (counts as 1 dc), dc2tog, dc in each st to 2 sts before side seam, [dc in side seam] twice, dc2tog, dc in each st to 2 sts before side seam, dc2tog, dc in side seam, join with sl st to 3rd ch of beg ch. Fasten off.

Rnd 2 Join B, work same as rnd 1, dec 2 sts at sides.

With C, work 1 rnd sc, 1 rnd dc.

With A, *work 1 rnd sc, 2 rnds dc*, place marker in last rnd; rep from * to *. Fasten off.

Fold to inside along marked rnd and sew to form casing, leaving approx 2"/5cm open. Thread elastic through casing, adjust to fit, then sew ends of elastic tog. Sew casing closed.

AVIATOR HELMET

TOOLKIT

YARN (4) • 3½oz/100g, 150yd/230m of any worsted weight wool blend.

HOOK • Size G/6 (4.5mm) crochet hook *or size to obtain gauge*

Finished Measurements
Head circumference 20"/51 cm.
Depth 7¼"/18.5 cm.

Gauge
5 mesh pats and 7 rnds = 4"/10cm over dc mesh pat. *Take time to check gauge.*

Helmet
Beg at top edge, ch 5, join with sl st to first ch to form ring.
Rnd 1 Work 12 sc in ring, join with sl st to first sc.
Rnd 2 Ch 4 (counts as 1 dc and ch 1), *1 dc in next sc, ch 1; rep from * around, join with sl st to 3rd ch of ch-4. **Rnd 3** Ch 3 (counts as 1 dc), 2 dc in first ch-1 space, *3 dc in next ch-1 space; rep from * around, join to top of ch-3—twelve 3-dc (groups) or mesh.
Rnds 4 and 5 Rep rnd 3.
Inc rnd 6 Ch 3, 2 dc in first ch-1 space, *(3 dc, ch 1, 3 dc) in next ch-1 space (for inc), 3 dc in next ch-1 space; rep from * 4 times more, inc in last ch-1 space—18 mesh.
Rnds 7–9 Work even on 18 mesh.
Inc rnd 10 Ch 3, 2 dc in first ch-1 space, *3 dc in next ch-1 space, inc in next ch-1 space, 3 dc in next ch-1 space; rep from * 4 times more, 3 dc in next ch-1 space, inc in last ch-1 space—24 mesh.
Rnds 11–14 Work even on 24 mesh.
Work Earflaps
Rnd 15 Ch 3, 2 dc in first ch-1 space, work 4 more mesh, turn. **Next row** Ch 3, 2 dc in first ch-1 space, work 3 more mesh, turn. **Next row** Ch 3, 2 dc in first ch-1 space, work 2 more mesh, turn. **Next row** Ch 3, 2 dc in first ch-1 space, work 1 more mesh, turn.
Last row Ch 3, 2 dc in first ch-1 space. Fasten off. Skip 5 mesh (for back of helmet), re-join yarn and work the 2nd earflap as for the first, do not fasten off at end.

Finishing
Working around the entire lower edge of helmet, work 3 rnds of sc evenly around lower edge. Cut 12 strands of yarn to fit the 27"/68.5 cm around the lower edge of helmet plus several extra inches/cm for braiding. Braid tog and sew braid around lower edge of helmet. Cut 12 strands of yarn 25"/63.5 cm long and attach with a knot for braid tie to earflap tip. Braid and knot. Trim ends.

Radius Pictures